Not All Is Good But Good Comes From All

radiant appearances perfectly expressed

NOT ALL IS GOOD
BUT
GOOD COMES FROM ALL

Radiant

Appearances

Perfectly

Expressed

Thelma J. Hembroff

copyright © 2005 Easy Times Press
17306 Northchapel Street
Spring, Texas 77379

www.annegillis.com
anne@annegillis.com
800-711-4580

Printed in the U.S. by instantpublisher.com

ISBN: 0-9662874-3-6

This book is dedicated in memory
and honor of my mother,

Esther Iva
Thompson-Stoppleworth-Bredeson

Table of Contents

ACKNOWLEDGEMENTS

The love that flows between people is just one of God's many gifts to humankind. I have experienced the joy of that gift with so many of you in this lifetime, and it would not be possible to acknowledge all of you individually. I will list just a few of you by name. However, whether we met once and shared a smile of friendship, or if we have known each other for years, may you know that I value the gift of love that we shared.

My mother,
Esther Iva Thompson-Stoppleworth-Bredeson.

My brothers and sisters –
Evelyn Erlene Stoppleworth Mehlhoff,
Kenneth Francis Stoppleworth,
Thomas Frank Stoppleworth,
Lois Faye Stoppleworth Sam,
and Mark Everett Stoppleworth.

My children,
David Wayne Hembroff and
Janine Kae Kietlow.
Thanks for choosing me to be your mother. I am so proud to be a part of your lives.

And also: Anne, Cyd and Fran, my Master Mind buddies, who helped me to create everyday miracles; Barbara Clark and Marilyn Opp, my prayer partners; my other prayer partners, too numerous to mention (and you know who you are); Naomi Bourne, master editor and typesetter, who worked closely with me for many hours to bring my story to print; Regina Bailey-Rehberg, graphic artist, for her beautiful cover design; Pat McHenry, who helped in the early stages by transcribing my thoughts; Helen Jaseph and Linda Nash, for their proofreading and encouragement. Thank you for all your help, and thank you for being part of this wonderful project.

Thelma J. Hembroff
June 2005

FOREWORD

Thelma and I are life buddies. We met in Memphis, Tennessee at a time when we both served New Thought churches. She graciously assisted me in the structural reorganization of my church. While other ministers may have seen my endeavor as competition, Thelma supported me without reserve.

Although support is wonderful, action is even better. Thelma helped me to write the by-laws of my church and was there for me in many other aspects of my ministry. One of the most challenging events for a minister is helping others to cope with death, and Thelma shared with me her unique way to conduct a funeral service. I often called her to ask, "What are you speaking about this Sunday?" and then gleaned ideas for my own Sunday message. When my church grew and we moved to a larger location — Thelma was there. She sent a huge plant to our grand opening and befriended me as I moved through the joys and problems of service.

Thelma has always been a rebel. She has a gift for putting people with opposing ideologies at the same table of life. She promotes diversity and speaks openly about controversial topics. I often watched her leave people squirming as she espoused her sane (but not always popular) views on life. The dynamic message she speaks and lives is this:

- We are responsible for our lives.

- We can choose our experience of life regardless of what happened to us.

- Power is carried in words.

- Nothing short of tolerance and compassion towards other religions, cultures and races is acceptable.

Our most powerful relationship came in the form of prayer partners. Thelma and I, along with Fran Pitman and Cyd Mosteller, met for more than 13 years as Master Mind partners. This form of fellowship and prayer was popularized in Napoleon Hill's book, *Think and Grow Rich*. It is similar to the Twelve Step process in recovery, except Master Mind partners use steps to share our dreams and goals. In this process, the Master Mind partners offer verbal support. The group was the foundational support that allowed us to live our missions. Jesus said, "Whenever two or more gather and ask — it shall be done." Well, we gathered and asked for years and years and watched miracle after miracle unfold. This book represents the blossoming of one of the seeds planted in those prayers.

Thelma moved away from Memphis not too

long before me. We seem to live parallel lives. We cry over the same things, laugh together and always hold the highest thoughts for each other. We had similar ministries in the same town and even started and left our churches around the same time. God is always saying to the two of us: "You are sisters, stay in touch; and always love and support each other."

When Thelma told me she was ready to write her book, I was so excited. I supported her vision in every way. I told her it would be easy. That wasn't completely honest, but I knew if she worked the project one day at a time, she could do it. I promised to publish her book, and sent her to my miracle editor. People often want to write books, but seldom get past the first few chapters. More often than not, they never even start. I believed in Thelma's story and wanted her to write it. I did whatever I could to get her started on the project, knowing how easy it would be in her daily life (with the demands of church and personal life maintenance) to never write her book.

Now my sister shares her compelling spiritual journey. Can you imagine being born as the product of a rape? When I first learned about this years ago, my stomach turned. Most people would keep this on the QT, but Thelma openly shared her roots and shared how she overcame such a tragic beginning. Now her book offers inspiration for those who live the trials and magic of life. Her life shouts: There are no excuses! We are responsible and respond-able and no matter what happens, we can always have good lives. There is no problem or circumstance that does not serve as a stepping stone to our higher good. Her life is truly a demonstration of the principle: *Not all things are good, but good comes from all.*

Thelma uses her personal story to teach the larger truths and wisdom of life. You will not want to put the book down as you read about her life: growing up in a sod house on the North Dakota prairie; discovering the secret of her origin; losing her memory because of electric shock treatments; losing custody of her children because of her spiritual beliefs; and finally, receiving the gifts and miracles that spring from her world of faith, prayer and creative thought.

Easy Times Press is proud to offer the vulnerable tale and life-affirming story of the Reverend Thelma. J. Hembroff.

Anne Sermons Gillis
May 2005

INTRODUCTION

Did you look at the inside title page as you thumbed through this book? Did you notice the acronym formed by the first letter of each word of the subtitle? It's a four-letter word that evokes strong feelings in people. Did you feel fear or anger? Were you repelled, or were you curious as to why I chose that particular subtitle?

I was not raped. Rape happens to someone else, doesn't it? Usually it happens to a stranger, or sometimes to an acquaintance, but it rarely happens to someone you know.

Although I was not raped, my life was absolutely and completely affected by *a* rape. My mother was raped, and that was the beginning of life for me.

There is no way to avoid every difficulty that life presents. Some problems can be side-stepped, but never all. Why are some people devastated by adversity while others find the strength to transform the perceived negative events of their lives? People are different, and their coping skills are different. Environments make a difference, too — family, friends, urban or rural locations — it all makes a difference. The reaction to adversity can create self-imposed walls that imprison, or it can build bridges to new places. My role as a minister teaches me of the transformative power God's love has on perception.

Fairy tales begin with "Once upon a time...", and generally have a lesson attached. The events didn't happen, but we use the lessons in the story to reflect on own lives. What influences are you experiencing in the spiritual, emotional, mental or physical aspects of your life? What encouraged you to choose this book to read?

The following story — my story — exists because I was guided to share the experiences of my journey. The lessons experienced were for my soul's enlightenment, but perhaps they will shed some light on your life path. I write this book for those of you who want to build bridges, but don't know how.

Chapter 1

Beginning Again (Birth)

Once upon a time there was a baby girl born in a home for unwed mothers in Fargo, North Dakota. She was born to a woman who felt confused and conflicted about bearing this child. During the long months that the child's physical body grew in her womb, the essence of the child kindled love in the mother's heart. At the same time, the woman did not want her tiny angel girl, who was the result of rape.

Love triumphed, and the young mother committed herself to the child. The baby girl was born on a winter night with the umbilical cord wrapped around her neck. The first lesson that bonded the hearts of mother and child was that good comes from all. This brave woman chose to set aside the negative brand of the baby's origin. As for the baby girl, she had made commitments of her own at the soul level before being born.

When I was just a few weeks old, my maternal grandparents brought my mother and me to their home on the prairies of North Dakota. The drive was over one hundred miles each way, and the old car we rode in was propelled more through faith than through mechanics. The joy surrounding my birth was tempered by sadness. After all, what man would want my mother now that she had been shamed? Demonstrating their love of family by their actions, my grandparents accepted a destiny of helping to raise me in their home.

As I began to realize myself as a separate soul, a miracle happened. Just seven months after arriving at my new home, Mom married the man of her dreams. Prior to this time, my mother and her beloved were forbidden to marry. He was sent to California and she to Minnesota in order to separate them. It didn't work. Their feelings were so strong that not even my mother's rape could keep them apart. They married in September of the first year of my life, and my stepfather raised me as his own child. If my mother had not been raped, her parents would not have let her marry the man she dearly loved — another blessing. Without their marriage, none of my sisters or brothers would have been born. The blessings continue.

Memories

Lying in a crib in a dark-colored room is the earliest memory I have of living with my mother's parents, Thomas John and Alma Thompson. I was named Thelma Joanne for T. J., my grandfather's initials. I remember the wallpaper in my room as dark with big flowers all over it. Years later, I discussed with my mom how awful it was. Mom laughed and agreed, but after a long pause she said, "How could you remember that as a baby under one year of age?"

Then our family started to grow. Six brothers and sisters joined our family over the next eleven years. Evelyn was born just eighteen months after me. Kenneth, Lois, Thomas and Mark followed. I was eleven when Mark was born, and I took care of his needs, as though he was my own child. Our life was poor according to earthly standards, but my childhood was rich with love.

In later years, my mother became known as a prairie woman. She had lived in a sod house as a farmer's wife and raised six children. She could stretch a few dollars farther than humanly possible. Mom seemed to enjoy her rural life and big family, despite the hard work involved. She always smiled at her children when we came to her with disagreements. She never tried to figure out who was right or wrong, telling us, "You know how to solve your own problems." This taught us to be strong individuals.

My mother is gone now. At her request, I spoke at her memorial service. She wanted me to say, "Her children were her greatest gifts to the world." This made all of us, her children, even more proud of our mother.

NOT ALL IS GOOD, BUT
GOOD COMES FROM ALL.

Chapter 2

Illusion in a
Child's Mind

Life in North Dakota was not easy. The hardships of extreme weather — harsh winters and hot, dry summers — left a significant imprint on me. I had frequent dreams at night that provided visions of my future.

The dream of living in my grandparents' home was very vivid. My grandparents lived in a home much bigger than our sod house. The original owners purchased it from the Sears-Roebuck Catalogue for $800. An Evangelist named Billy Sunday gave the owners the money to build this house, so it was called the "Sunday Place." My grandparents bought the house and restored it. In my child's mind it was a mansion. A crystal chandelier hung in the dining room. In reality, it was just a fluorescent lamp with a string of crystals, but in my child's mind it was a grand chandelier. My dream was to live in this house.

Allow me to tell you about my grandfather Frank, my favorite person in the whole wide world. He was my hero, my sun and my savior. He purchased my very first store-bought dress for me. It was a beautiful blue dress with a white collar, and I wore it every chance I could.

My grandfather was a rather large man who always carried Sen-Sen (a licorice candy) with him. A delightful ritual was involved in distributing the candy to the six children. Each of us licked the palm of one hand, and he shook out a few pieces of Sen-Sen for each of us. The taste of sweet licorice lingered on our damp palms as we ate the treat. Even today, eating licorice candy brings me a feeling of love.

My grandfather was a land magnate who could never acquire enough land. He and my dad, along with lots of hired help, farmed all the acreage. The entire family worked on the farm. We had a dairy cow which Mom milked so we could have fresh milk, butter and cheese. My dad never liked the farm, but thought it was his duty to stay there and help out. Dad was never an equal partner in the farming venture. He did not learn to manage his money, as his father paid for things as needed. Dad was never given a salary. He didn't have a clue how to handle finances, run a farm, or pay a bill. He just worked very hard on the farm.

The death of my grandfather did not change that aspect of his life. He was always going to take care of paying the bills tomorrow. Dad threw the bills out of sight, in a drawer or wastebasket, whatever was convenient. To this day I carry the belief that when a bill comes in, I have to pay it that day or within the next two or three days. I never want to be known for not being able to pay my investments (otherwise called bills).

Our whole family was impacted when we received the news that my grandfather had died. I can remember the phone ringing in the middle of the night and asking my mother who was on the phone. She said grandpa had died. At that moment I believed I had caused his death because of the dreams I had about moving into the house. I stood screaming in terror and my mother had to slap my face to get my attention. Then she awakened the rest of my brothers and sisters.

We went to my grandparents' house to view the body before it was taken to the funeral home. Granddad was stretched out on the floor looking like he was asleep. We took turns saying goodbye to our grandfather before the hearse came to take him away. I reflected on my dream. In my limited understanding I thought I had caused his death. I didn't dare tell anybody because in my ten-year-old mind I thought I would go to jail. I carried this guilt until I was twenty-six years old.

Later we would live in the house I had dreamed of, but being happy there was difficult. I always wanted to keep the house clean like my grandparents kept it. Periodically the guilt would return reminding me that I caused my grandfather's death. A constant reminder of that belief happened when I had to clean the chandelier. Since I was the tallest child I cleaned the chandelier often.

I was so bonded to my grandfather that his influence reflected in the men I chose to put into my life. I even married two men very similar to him. Granddad was charming, generous, fun-loving and industrious. He made a positive impact on my life. In later years, however, I realized that he had also been a controlling, domineering person.

NOT ALL IS GOOD, BUT
GOOD COMES FROM ALL.

Chapter 3

My Childhood
Experiences

Early school experiences can imprint memories for us all. As the oldest child, I was the first to go off to school. Of all my early school memories, the most prominent one is from the first grade. My country school was three miles away, and I had to cross a pasture that contained a bull. I heard bulls would chase anyone wearing red. I only owned one coat, and it was red. I cried all the way to school and all the way home. In my mind, the bull was always breathing down my neck. I vomited many times on the way to and from school.

But I didn't tell my mother, and I tried to hide my tears from her. She had enough to deal with. I was just a little girl, but I was making adult decisions about not creating more hardships for my mother.

One day, my dad's father Frank picked me up at school. The teacher told him, "This child is not learning anything. She cries until noon. In the afternoon, she starts crying again. It's not possible for me to teach her under these conditions."

My grandfather became my hero that day. He convinced my parents to enroll me in a school in town. It meant that I lived in Woodworth with my maternal grandparents during the week. On the weekends, I went home, except when severe winter weather prevented it.

I was glad to leave the bull behind, but I missed my parents and the sod house in the country. The house was made from earth. The walls were so thick that I could curl up on a windowsill and sit in the sun.

There were no more trips across the pasture with the bull in it, but my grandfather couldn't protect me from the next "bull" in my life. The four-legged beast that I feared was replaced by a two-legged one. One of the teachers from the school in town always wanted me to sit on his lap. He would put his hand into my panties, and then give me a nickel.

I tried to avoid him, but he came to eat every day at the restaurant that my maternal grandparents owned. We lived upstairs above the restaurant. I was too young to know the word for what the teacher was doing, but of course he was molesting me.

In our small town, everyone thought this teacher was a nice man. My family thought I was being unfriendly. They didn't know what the teacher did, and I never told anyone. During Christmas break, this teacher was arrested in a nearby town for molesting children. I think he went to jail.

During that first year, I lived apart from my parents most of the time. In North Dakota, it snows frequently during the winter, and the drive home was too difficult to make. The next year, my parents moved into town to make going to school easier for all the children.

That first day of school, my sister and I were dressed alike in brand new striped t-shirts and bib overalls that my grandfather bought for us. Later, when my sister and I were called to the front of the room, I was sure it was because of our nice new clothes. A moment later, my pride turned to shame as the teacher said, "Overalls are not acceptable clothes for girls to wear. Anyone who comes to school looking like this will be punished."

That was the first of many painful days at school. Learning the ABC's came easily to me, but speaking them was a challenge. I stuttered so badly that I couldn't say my own name. All the kids laughed at me when I tried to read out loud in class. This reading grade on my report card was a big red F.

Although I tried, it was impossible to meet this teacher's expectations. I withdrew more deeply into my inner world, where I conversed happily with invisible friends. My secret friends never laughed at me, even though I failed reading because of my stutter.

Two of my mother's sisters were just five and seven years older than me. My aunts were like sisters to me and I spent a lot of time with them. One evening, we were at band practice together when the woman who taught first and second grade accused me of ruining the sound of the drums. This was the same teacher who embarrassed me the day I wore overalls. I didn't know what she was talking about. She called me a liar and slapped my face in front of everyone. In those days, children never talked back to a teacher, but it was many years before I was able to forgive her.

To cope with my anger, I imagined myself as a dentist with this teacher in my chair. I used a drill on her teeth, taking satisfaction from her pain. I have a vivid visual imagination, and this image was frequently in my mind. Later on, in my teenage years, I needed a lot of dental work. I brought suffering upon myself with the power of those vengeful thoughts, since thoughts (positive or negative) always manifest for the thinker.

Around that same time, I started growing very quickly. I got so weary of hearing people say what a nice big girl I was. My height drew too much attention at a time when I wanted to be invisible. Whenever people talked about my height, I concentrated on being small. Because of that, my height has not changed since fifth grade. Even without knowing or understanding mind power, the intensity of my thoughts stopped my growth.

In the third grade, I finally had a different teacher. My family had moved again, and two of my younger siblings were now school age. Along with a few neighbors, there were enough students to open a one-room country school. One teacher taught first through eighth grade. The only one in third grade with me was a boy who rode a horse to school. The teacher boarded at our house, so even during a blizzard, the children in my family didn't get a break from school. The dining room became our classroom.

By the fifth grade, my stuttering problem was in the past, thanks to a teacher who told me I could accomplish anything. She was patient and praised me for my success. Her love and support reassured me that I had worth. On a spiritual level, my years of stuttering had been an unlikely benefit. The extended silence it forced upon me gave me time to develop my connection with nature and God.

I remember painful things about my stuttering years. When I lived with my grandparents, I ate at their restaurant after school. Pies were baked fresh every day, so if any were left over, I had my choice for a snack. My favorite pie was pumpkin, but that was too hard to say, so I always asked for apple. I was afraid people would laugh at my stuttering. The hardest fear to overcome was the fear of people laughing at me. Fear is a great teacher. Today, apple is my least favorite pie.

Another pivotal life change came as the result of my grandfather's death. At age ten, I was not prepared for death. My father moved us to Oregon soon after that. It was a great culture shock. Our family of eight, plus my grandmother, drove across the country in a Buick. My dad went to work in the sawmills with his brother and our family lived at my uncle's home.

I loved living in Oregon and living with my

cousins. My uncle and his wife had four children. Some of the children had rooms in the garage, which was separate from the house. This gave us a great deal of freedom. We used to smuggle the toaster, bread and cocoa out to our rooms in the middle of the night.

My cousin dreamed up pranks for us to do. Some nights we strung toilet paper across the bridge near the house. We hid under the bridge and laughed when we heard the cars slam on their brakes. In the darkness, the paper looked like a solid barrier. Choice words were heard from the drivers.

Our family raised banty chickens, a colorful breed that laid small eggs. One night, my cousin and I snuck out to the coop and pulled the chickens' tails. Someone at the house heard the racket, so we ran up the side of the mountain. Later we found out it was our fathers with shotguns — they thought skunks had gotten into the coop! We could have been shot.

The next morning, my aunt questioned us. She suspected that there were two-legged skunks out that night. My cousin and I thought we were getting away with these escapades, but we rarely did.

My cousins, brothers, sisters and me rode a school bus to the local school. The bus waited for us at the end of the driveway every school morning. One morning, no children came out of the garage when it was time for school. One of the boys was sent to get us. We were barely conscious, and had to be carried out. The gas fumes from a malfunctioning heater almost took our lives. After we were fully conscious, our parents poured coffee into us to keep us awake. We all had headaches and were throwing up. I guess it wasn't time for us to leave this world.

I hardly cracked a book the whole time I was in sixth grade in Oregon. I had learned everything they taught while attending class at that one-room schoolhouse in North Dakota. However, I did discover boys. Sometimes we held hands when we went to the movies. Those were the days, my friends. Other times, my cousin smuggled me onto the bus when the high school band played at out-of-town basketball games. The thrill of spending time with the older teenagers was intense.

This exciting year came to an end when it was time to return to North Dakota to put in the spring crops. I still love the mountains, because of my joyous experiences in Oregon.

Back at the one-room schoolhouse, it took some work to catch up on what we hadn't been taught in Oregon. I wanted to appear so grown up at this time, and decided that smoking cigarettes was one way to act older. I went to the outhouse and smoked a cigarette taken from my dad. One day, one of the younger kids smelled tobacco on my breath. I was proud to reveal my secret. They wanted to try it too, but I said smoking was only for grown-ups like me.

My know-it-all attitude knew no limits. I asked the teacher one day if we could sit in her car to talk. I didn't think of her as my superior. After all, she had just graduated from high school. In those days, a country schoolteacher didn't need a college degree or experience. She sat down and lit her cigarette. After I sat down next to her, I lit one, too. Though obviously shocked, she never said a thing.

One day, I was off in the field having a smoke when I was supposed to be watching my brothers and sisters. During my absence, my brother hurt himself. When I heard him crying, I ran to the house. Mom was there, and she smelled tobacco on my breath. She told me in no uncertain terms that I was *not* grown up, I was not to smoke anymore, and I should consider myself lucky that she wasn't going to tell Dad.

My behavior didn't change — I just got wiser about selecting a time and place to smoke. Sometimes I crawled out on the roof from my bedroom at night to smoke after everyone else was sleeping. Brushing my teeth took care of the odor.

I knew it wasn't good to smoke. In high school, I decided to play basketball, and gave up cigarettes without a second thought. The coach told us not to smoke, and although I was just a moderate player, I took the game seriously. One year, our team finished in second place in the State Championship.

I started working at the age of nine doing anything to earn money for school clothes. Some of my jobs included baby-sitting, painting fences, and painting houses inside and out. The farmers often called on me to be their "gopher," to go for

16

this and that in town.

I even picked wool. My family always had a flock of sheep, perhaps six hundred or more in the pasture. During the winter, a few sheep would die. In the spring, we children hiked out to the pasture. While positioned upwind from the maggot-infested body, we removed the wool from the dead sheep, put it in a sack and took it to town to sell.

In North Dakota, there was a large gopher population, and each gopher tail was worth a few cents. We caught plenty. In the winter months, another way to make money was from a trap-line that my dad set for muskrats. Muskrats build their dam-like houses on top of the ice with a hole under the frozen lake. By chopping a hole in its house one can put a trap in. When Dad felt he had exhausted the supply of muskrats, he would turn the line over to us children. We checked the traps while walking to school in the morning. Any dead animals we brought to school stayed frozen outside, since the temperature was often below zero.

As a teenager, my focus broadened to include people as well as money. We lived about eight miles outside a little town and I was always looking for reasons to go to town. I cooked Mom's recipe for lefsa, a Norwegian delicacy, to sell at church. My draw to the church at that time wasn't spiritual — I just wanted to be in town. Every summer, I volunteered to teach Bible school. I did almost anything to get off the farm and socialize.

Except for one store-bought dress, all of my clothes were hand-me-downs. My parents could not afford to buy new clothes. I fondly remember a high school teacher who lived with us on the farm when I was in high school. She shared my room. Her whole paycheck went to purchasing clothes that she saw in catalogs. She let me wear her clothes first before hemming them to fit her short stature. In this way, I manifested new clothes.

During hunting season our home became the stopping point for duck hunters from many states. Mom cooked for the hunters and I was the hunting guide. In addition to showing the hunters where the ducks were, I cleaned and froze the ducks for them. In exchange, I got to drive the hunters' big cars! I started driving at age nine, and obtained my driver's license at eleven. Because I drove cars, trucks, and tractors, the hunters trusted me with their fancy cars.

In high school, I preferred social interaction with my teachers instead of classmates my own age, who seemed immature. As a freshman, I was chosen to be in the junior-senior play, so I spent a lot of time with the older students. When they went out at night to drink, I was the designated driver, so I never drank in high school.

On my sixteenth birthday at dinner, I was so embarrassed when one of my sisters asked, "Can Thelma start dating now?" My father glared at me and grumbled, "I guess so." When a boy finally asked to take me to a movie, I remember feeling intense fear. He drove a long way to pick me up at the farm. Of course, he came in the house to greet my parents. Everyone knew each other in this small community, so no introductions were needed. It was awkward, and we left the house quickly.

It was about twenty miles back to town and the movie theatre. There was time to spare before the movie started, so we detoured a few miles to Spiritwood Lake, where he kissed me. I must confess this wasn't my first date. It was just the first one my parents were aware of.

Dating by association was the norm for me. When I accompanied my aunts, they arranged a date for me. They wanted to be with their boyfriends and not have me as excess baggage. One night, I started to cry when I learned who my companion was going to be, so my aunts made different arrangements.

It was during this time in high school that I sensed a secret was being kept from me. In my search to discover this secret, I began an adventure — meeting other people. There was no e-mail and no internet, only pen pals. At age sixteen, without telling my parents, I put an ad for a pen pal in a magazine. The ad I wrote said: five-foot-two, eyes of blue, and so on, but I never revealed my age. Soon I was getting dozens of letters every day. I finally had to tell my mother about the ad when I received marriage proposals from older men — at age sixteen, most of them seemed old to me.

I continued to correspond with two pen pals into my adult years. One was in the Navy and the other in the Army. One man wanted to send me gifts from Japan, but Mom wouldn't allow it. He wrote to my mother, explaining that he was an alcoholic who would drink up the money if he didn't spend it on gifts. After my mother gave her permission, I received beautiful gifts from a man I never met. Giving to me was a benefit to him. Years later, a Navy man who lived in our vicinity returned home with a message for me. It was a blessing from the "gift man" wanting to thank me for accepting the gifts.

The other man was in the Army. He stopped writing to me after I got married. I often wonder what happened to these two men. Out of the hundreds of letters and photographs that I received, these two men stand out in my mind as very dear souls. Wherever you are — accept my blessings. I pray for both of you that your lives have been good.

NOT ALL IS GOOD, BUT
GOOD COMES FROM ALL.

Chapter 4

Discovery of
Old Secrets

Have you ever felt like every person around you was keeping a secret and you were the only one who didn't know what it was? To this day, I don't deal well with secrets. I don't like surprise birthday parties, unopened gifts or any other kind of surprise. Throughout my school years, everyone seemed to know this secret. It was about me, but no one was willing to tell me what it was. It seemed like the secret would never be revealed, and the waiting would never end.

There signals were subtle, but real. One time, as a child, I was looking at photographs of my parents' wedding, and I asked, "Where am I?" My aunt replied, "Someone was taking care of you in the school house." Although I asked no more questions, her reply never left my mind — because I shouldn't have been born yet. The fragment of truth shouted out to me that there was much more to know. It was torment to hear kids at school say to my brothers and sisters, "You know, she's not your *real* sister."

During my senior year in high school, I wrote to the Bureau of Vital Statistics in Bismarck, North

Dakota for my birth certificate. I sent three dollars of my hard-earned baby-sitting money, along with my mother's name and address. Then I told my mother that a letter was coming with her name and address on it, but she should not open it because it was something for my social studies project.

A few weeks later, the letter arrived. I went to my room and held the envelope, afraid to open it. What I would see might change the course of my life. After a deep breath, I gingerly tore the envelope and took out the contents. Low and behold, my birth certificate was in my hands! With a pounding heart and closed eyes, I held it for a long time before looking at it. My first reaction was that I surely did have a lot of names — a total of six, not just Thelma Joanne Stoppleworth. Next I looked for my father's name, but the space was empty. Who was my father? I knew about the cabbage patch and finding babies under the leaves, but I didn't look like a cabbage leaf. Although what I read was a shock, it explained my inner-knowing that there really was a secret.

No tears came, but I hadn't taken a full breath since I started reading. My mind was swirling. My search for answers just raised more questions. Why did I have six names on the birth certificate? My name was spelled different ways: Joan and Joanne. For the rest of the day, I went about my normal chores, not knowing how to talk to my mother. I wanted her full attention, but there were so many chores to do on the farm, like feeding the chickens, watering the garden, pulling weeds, fixing dinner and doing dishes.

It seemed like forever before Mom finished her evening chores. Finally, the time seemed right. I asked Mom if she could come to my room. I closed the door behind us, and felt the tension rise within me as I handed her my birth certificate. Mom's face turned pale and she started to cry. "We always meant to tell you. We meant to have Dad adopt you."

The story she told me was beyond anything I had every imaged about my origins. My mother had been raped. For several months, Mom had worked as a live-in domestic for a middle class family in Minnesota. One night, their son took my mother for a ride in his car. He was drunk, and he drove her many miles out into the country on roads that were rarely traveled. My mother never left the family's residence so she was totally lost.

Then came the ultimatum that began my life. "Put out or walk home," he threatened. She was more afraid of being left alone in that remote location than she was of his sexual advances. Mom thought the discomfort would only last a few minutes. She chose to remain, and endured a violent rape in the back seat of the car. She never imagined the violation of her body would affect her whole life. During the assault, Mom's rapist threatened her — if she told anyone, he would hurt her again.

The physical and mental abuse terrorized my mother, so she kept working for the family and kept the rape a secret. She soon realized this was a mistake. Her menstrual cycle didn't come, and she feared the worst. The man who raped her didn't

23

care. "That's not my problem," he said, when she told him about missing her cycle. "I'm engaged to be married, and you can't prove anything."

In those days, DNA testing didn't exist. Mom suffered in silence until her thickening waistline gave her away. Her employer figured out that Mom's flu was really morning sickness. When my mother revealed who the father was, her employer accused her of lying and fired her.

After that, Mom lived in a group home for unwed mothers in Fargo, North Dakota. She was put to work sewing for me, her unborn baby. If she chose to, she could give me up for adoption. During her pregnancy, Mom did not want me, which was understandable. After being forced to submit to a violent act, Mom was left with a person growing within her. Her condition was a constant reminder of that terrible event.

As we now know, my mother decided to keep me, her baby. After telling me all of this, Mom tried to reassure me that things didn't change just because I now knew the secret. Although he wasn't my biological father, she said, the man who had raised me as his daughter loved me.

No words could alter my confusion and resentment. Knowing the secret about my conception raised so many questions in my mind. I wondered if my stepfather loved my mother and me. I thought about the ways he treated me differently than my brothers and sisters. I was the only one of the children who never got a spanking from him. Was it because I behaved better, or because I wasn't his real child?

As a senior in high school, demonstrating a rebellious nature was the norm. Now that I knew my life began as a violent assault, I became even more rebellious, believing that I was excess baggage. I didn't listen to anything my stepfather said to me — after all, he wasn't my dad. Just two weeks after graduating from high school, I decided to leave home.

NOT ALL IS GOOD, BUT
GOOD COMES FROM ALL.

Chapter 5

The In-Between Years

I enrolled in an airline school in Minneapolis. Dad had to borrow money to pay for the tuition, and I vowed to repay him for that. A Jewish family provided my room and board in trade for babysitting, housecleaning and cooking. They also paid me five dollars a week. Half of that was spent on transportation to school.

My first venture with this airline school was flying from Jamestown, North Dakota to Minneapolis, Minnesota — a big deal at that time. I made some great friends, but this was my first extended stay away from home. During the first two weeks, I lost ten pounds and cried myself to sleep every night. When I wrote to Mom, telling her how I felt, she encouraged me to stick it out. One night, I called home collect, and Mom said I could come home. My uncle would give me a job in the post office. I heard myself say, "No, I *will* stay." I repeated it again with great emphasis, "I will stay."

It was my destiny to cut the ties and go on with my life. After that phone call and decision, I adjusted more readily to school, being away from

27

home and living in a city that seemed like the largest place in the world. This was a major change from being a prairie girl. One of my hopes was to discover who my biological father was. I had a name for him, but I did not pursue the mystery further — I was afraid of what I would learn.

A man I had known since my childhood moved to Minneapolis to be near me. When I was eight, and he not much older, he paid my brothers and sisters twenty-five cents per picture for photographs of me. He had always been infatuated with me.

I wrote to him two or three times when he was in the Army. He was stationed in Germany for a while, and was briefly engaged to the general's daughter.

Upon his release from the Army, this man pursued our relationship. He attended school during the day and worked nights. Since he had a car, he often drove me and my classmates around town when we needed transportation.

A few months later, he brought up marriage. The year was 1958. We talked about a summer wedding in July of the following year. Prior to the mid-1960's, the roles of men and women in relationships were more strictly defined. Men were very much in charge. Although I loved this man, I tried to break off the relationship several times because he was very jealous and possessive. He also kept a weapon in his car. I was afraid of what he might do if he became emotional.

We stayed together, but I insisted that he convert to the Lutheran faith before the wedding. This was the denomination in which I had been baptized and confirmed as a child. After completing some classes, he became a member of the Lutheran church.

Instead of waiting for summer, we decided to run away. We needed a marriage license, but my fiancé had spent all his money paying for a speeding ticket. He borrowed five dollars to pay for the license. Usually, there was a three-day waiting period for a license. The judge waived that requirement because he called our minister, who confirmed that we were both Lutheran and attending classes for engaged couples.

After the license was issued, I called my parents. They convinced us to postpone our plans so the family could be a part of the wedding.

We wanted to be married in Wahpeton, North Dakota, a small town near the state's southeastern corner. My aunt and uncle lived there, so it would be a convenient place for the family to gather. It was a surprise to find out that the marriage license was only valid in the state where it was issued -- Minnesota. Getting married was more complicated than we had imagined. Finally, Breckenridge was picked as the location for the wedding. It is just across the Red River from Wahpeton, in Minnesota. My aunt and uncle arranged for a church wedding for us on Valentine's Day in 1959. I was only a year out of high school.

The trip from Minneapolis to Wahpeton is about 200 miles. We left late in the evening, after my fiancé returned from work. My roommate was also my close friend, so she rode with us. It was snowing. The drive quickly turned into an adventure, since we traveled during one of the biggest snowstorms of the century. The roads became treacherous, and we drove slowly.

I was in the back seat, trying to sleep, but my fiancé and my roommate were in the front, singing and laughing. They were having a grand old time, and I was getting irritated. All of a sudden I heard, "We're out of gas. We have to find a gas station."

This happened just as we came upon a small town. The surrounding area was rural farmland for many miles. The headlights revealed footsteps in the snow, which we followed to a house. The homeowner was so helpful. Apparently there was only one gas station in the town, and it was closed. This kind man contacted the station owner, who opened up late at night just so we could get gas. Then we were on our merry way. By this time I was more than irritated — I was angry. Strangely, my car mates were still cheerful and having a great time. Why was I feeling this way?

And then it was my wedding day. My aunt loaned me a lovely navy blue suit to wear. There were still some last minutes details that needed attention. The women headed to the church in Breckenridge, and the men went to pick up flowers.

Hours went by. There were no flowers, no

groom, no wedding. My aunt's baby girl was screaming the whole time. The minister was getting ready to leave — he couldn't wait any longer.

I didn't know what to think. Was my fiancé having a good old time at an impromptu bachelor party? Why was everything surrounding this wedding so star-crossed? Just then, the men arrived. I was relieved and angry at the same time. It turned out there had been a car accident. No one was hurt, but my uncle's car was damaged.

I cried through the entire ceremony, and so did my aunt's baby. The baby had a reason — the nylon dress she wore irritated her skin, and she had a rash. The reason for my tears would be repressed for years.

Everyone drove back to Wahpeton for a big dinner. Between wedding gifts and money borrowed from my family, we newlyweds had enough money to pay for a hotel room. My aunt and uncle found space in their tiny home for my roommate, so my new husband and I had our privacy. That night at the hotel is still a vivid memory for me, because someone left the bar yelling "Zorro!" and sketched "Z" over and over in the snowy parking lot.

The next morning, after breakfast with the family, we headed back to Minneapolis. It was time to find a place of our own.

NOT ALL IS GOOD, BUT
GOOD COMES FROM ALL.

31

Chapter 6

Transforming
My Life

My new husband and I rented an apartment with a Murphy bed, which folds out of a cabinet attached to the wall. My husband went to school during the day and worked at night. I expected to finish airline school and begin working as a stewardess.

Instead, I encountered some of the prejudice against women that was typical of the late 1950's. There was also a prejudice against blondes. The company suggested that I let my hair go back to its natural color. As a natural blonde, that was not something I could change. When the airline company found out I was getting married they informed me that stewardesses were required to be single. After graduation, I found myself unemployed.

Eventually I found a job, and it was walking distance from the apartment so there were no transportation problems. Of the five women who were my classmates (and who paid to attend stewardess school) only one became an airline stewardess.

When my husband graduated from school he accepted a job with Boeing in Seattle, Washington. We packed all of our possessions into our car and left for Seattle, treating the trip as our honeymoon. With little money to spend on food, we purchased fresh fruit along the road for meals. As we crossed the floating bridge that signaled our arrival in Seattle, I started to cry. It felt like I was coming home. I never thought I would leave that city which I loved so much.

We lived in the suburbs for a while, and didn't know anyone. To save money, we rented a little apartment above a grocery store. I accepted a job at a local department store near a bus stop.

When I was growing up, I said I was never going to have any children. Who wanted them after being the oldest in a family of six children? It seemed like I was always the one to diaper, feed, dress, clean up after, wash and hang clothes outside in the heat of the summer sun or in the freezing winter cold. In the winter, the sheets would literally freeze dry. All the clothes required ironing, and the iron wasn't electric — it was heated on the back of a wood burning range. It took considerable care not to scorch the clothes. The shirts and dresses had to be heavily starched, sprinkled, rolled up and brought out one at a time to iron. There were no spray bottles to moisten the clothes. Cooking, cleaning and other chores seemed never to be finished with all the farm hands and kids to be cared for.

At first, my husband and I agreed that we didn't want children. But after a while, my husband decided he wanted children very much, and I conceded. We set aside the precautions, but I didn't become pregnant. I used special diets, positions, and timing according to my cycle and went to the doctor for many tests. Finally, my tubes were opened by a process that used air, and I was able to conceive.

It was an exciting time filled with changes. The little apartment was no longer suitable. After some searching, we finally found a two-bedroom brick house for $13,500 that the owner agreed to finance. Back then, that was a lot of money for a young couple.

We were a very social family. On the day the baby chose to make his arrival, we planned to have a couple over for dinner and a game of cards. I cleaned the house and prepared homemade pizza. I also called my obstetrician to ask about getting a prescription. I had wet my panties while standing at the kitchen sink, and hoped there was a pill I could take to prevent the leaking. It would be embarrassing to stand up from the dinner table or the card table with a wet bottom. The doctor told me to come into the office. It was looking as though the party would be delayed.

We only had the one car, so I waited for my husband to come home. The doctor was gone by the time we arrived, but he left a message on the door instructing me to go to the hospital for an examination. At the hospital, a nurse checked me and said, "Girl, you are in labor." It was thirty days before my due date, and I wanted to go home, but the doctor on call insisted that I check in immediately. Then he left, believing that it would be several hours before the baby's delivery. He no sooner arrived home than he received a call to come back to the hospital.

My husband walked into the delivery room wearing green hospital scrubs and joked, "We can begin — Ben Casey has arrived." Ben Casey was a popular television show, with a handsome doctor as the star of the show. As a rule, men were not permitted in the delivery room in those years. Before 1962, delivery procedures in hospitals were different. I didn't know it then, but the doctor and the hospital were very innovative for their time.

There was a mirror positioned so I could watch the whole miracle take place. Even though my mother had six children, she never discussed childbirth with me. I did not have a painful labor — I only remember five pains. I gave birth on March 9, 1962 to a son, weighing seven pounds and one ounce. Although he arrived a month early, my son was very healthy. I was glad to have his father in the room sharing this very special moment. Following my son's birth, he was placed on my stomach. When I touched his head with its matted-down hair, I fell in love with my wonderful son. His head was misshaped and his nose a bit smashed. He had been positioned head down, pressing on my pubic bone, so he didn't look very pretty, but was ever so lovable. This was definitely the most beautiful child ever born, even though his hospital picture didn't show it.

While I was pregnant, my son-to-be was referred to as Michael. Whenever relatives called, they asked, "How is Michael?" When my husband came home from work, he would ask, "How is Michael?" It was the name we had chosen. When the nurse brought my son into the room so I could sign the birth certificate, a little voice said to me, "His name is David." I looked around the room to see if anyone else was in the room. I wanted to hold the baby for a bit before signing the certificate. When I had my son cradled in my arms, I started to call him Michael. He seemed to speak to me, saying, "My name is David." I gasped, stared at him and said the name, "David." His body responded when I said that name. After the nurse took him back to the nursery, I wrote David Wayne Hembroff on the birth certificate. David and his father would share a middle name. Even though I complied with my son's request, I called him Michael for almost three weeks. Each time, I received a message from him saying, "My name is David."

David was born with at least two inches of long hair standing straight up on his head. In his first picture, his hair looked like a broken-open straw bale. I remember putting mineral oil on his hair to help it lay flat.

As a new mother, I was excited about nursing my baby. I wanted to be all that a mother is supposed to be, but my body wasn't cooperating with the project. When my mother came to help me, I found out that I didn't have enough milk to nurse. Mom said, "A skinny old cow doesn't milk very well either." I fed David substitute milk because he was allergic to cow's milk.

A few months later, I went back to work. During the day, David stayed with a baby-sitter. Although my son was a joy, he was also a very curious young man. His exploring included anywhere he could climb or anywhere he could crawl. One time I found him on top of the refrigerator. I caught my breath, reached up high over my head, and took down a smiling, triumphant child who was proud of his accomplishments. David had pushed his high chair against the kitchen counter and used it as a ladder to get on the counter. Then he put one canister on top of the other and climbed on this wobbly foundation to end up on top of the refrigerator. Another time I found David in the fireplace covered with ashes. His white teeth glimmered through his soot-covered face. He was happy even though he was a big mess.

When David was nine months old, the three of us moved to Fairbanks, Alaska. Three days later, David was in the hospital with an ear infection. During the year we lived in Alaska, David was hospitalized nine times. When he was very ill, we flew him to Anchorage or Seattle for treatment. The specialist in Seattle met us at the airport. After several days in the Seattle hospital, David recovered. Within seven days of returning to Alaska, he would be sick again. I believed there was something wrong with Alaska. The last time this happened, I decided to leave Alaska permanently.

My husband took a leave of absence from work. We packed everything into our Volkswagen Beetle and the three of us headed for Seattle via the Alcan Highway, which at that time was a dried-up riverbed. In Seattle, David was immediately hospitalized. A mastoid ear operation removed all of the apparatus from his left ear, leaving him permanently deaf in that ear. Fortunately, the infection had not spread to the brain. Tests later revealed that my husband was a carrier of the staph infection, so Alaska was innocent after all.

I was cast as the "bad" mom who helped to hold David during the many procedures needed to care for his ears before, during and after the operation. He was often wrapped up like a mummy to restrain him while the doctors worked. I have always felt that David carried unconscious resentment for me, the source of his pain and anguish. He looked so healthy as a child. No one would guess the health issues he faced in the first years of his life. David was quite a little trooper who cried briefly and then bounced back to his happy self again.

The house in Seattle was rented during our time in Alaska, so we moved back into it. It was a two-bedroom brick house with a single car garage on a large lot in a nice neighborhood. My husband found a new job in the city, working a lot of overtime so we could make ends meet. We installed a chain-link fence so David could play safely in the backyard on the play set and in the sandbox. All types of roses and other flowering plants grew around the house. My husband loved yard work and gardening, and had quite a green thumb. He felt very connected and peaceful when he worked in the earth. I believe he inherited his love of nature from one of his ancestors, who was a Canadian Algonquin Indian.

During the time in Alaska, when David was always sick, my husband talked about wanting another child. I agreed to have another child if we left Alaska permanently. A little over two years later, that time arrived. Just like David, our precious baby daughter was born thirty days early on July 19th, 1964; she weighed six pounds and four ounces.

The events preceding this birth were very similar to those that happened before David was born. With both pregnancies, I never had a day of morning sickness or any discomfort. I enjoyed the glow of that special time, and never felt the need to modify my activities. The day before my daughter was born was filled with major activities. My husband and I painted the dining room and living room, moved furniture, re-hung pictures on the walls, took David to a baby-sitter, and went to a company picnic that began around noon. After lunch, I even played softball. Some of the employees brought alcohol to the picnic, and one very drunk man wanted to go for a walk with me along the river. Either I didn't look pregnant, or he was extremely drunk. I felt huge, but actually during my pregnancy with David, I only gained eighteen pounds; with my daughter, just eleven pounds. After the company picnic, we had dinner with some friends. By this time, I really wasn't with the program. Everyone else was having fun, but I was tired.

The next morning, I couldn't stop going to the bathroom. It took some effort to track down my doctor. When I called my doctor's office, the staff told me he was at the hospital. But when I called the hospital, he wasn't there either. They gave me the number of a different hospital to call. My doctor started to say, "Wait for contractions." Then he remembered my prior delivery without labor pains. Even though I wasn't registered at that hospital, my doctor instructed me to come over immediately. "You get here now," he said.

When the nurse laid this perfect baby girl, Janine Kae, on my tummy, I touched her smooth pink skin, experienced her sweetness for the first time and I fell in love. With tears in my eyes, I looked at her with awe. She was much smaller at birth than David. The roundness and perfect shape of her face was a sign that birth was easier for her. Positioned differently in my body, Janine was born with an appearance that was soft, sweet, gentle and loving.

Janine liked to cuddle and be held really close, looking up at my face with her beautiful blue eyes. Her hair was a soft blonde, very manageable and fun to work with. When I nursed her, she wanted more contact time. A happy child in the morning, she always greeted me with a smile and giggle and reached out to me, so I could lift her out of her crib. She loved everyone and never met a stranger. When we went shopping together, Janine always won the hearts of people and would bring her new friends to meet me.

Janine learned to walk at seven months, which was quite astonishing. At one of her check-ups, the doctor called the staff over to witness her ability.

Janine was so small that she literally walked under the doctor's desk. Right around that time, she began to have problems with her eyes. It was obvious — Janine was cross-eyed. At the age of nine months, she had her first eye surgery. Another surgery followed when she was about two years old. One thing was certain — her tiny face looked adorable in glasses.

According to the storybooks, my life was perfect: You get married, have children, and live happily ever after. I was supposed to be happy. My life was filled with friends and wonderful events, but I felt empty and unfulfilled. Before I became pregnant with Janine, I asked my husband if we could go for marriage counseling. He thought we had a perfect marriage. If something was wrong, it must be my own problem. He said I could see a counselor if I paid for it myself.

My discontent continued after Janine was born and again I wanted us to see a counselor, but my husband's reply was the same. Our friends said we were a perfect couple. I went into a deep depression, which was related to post-partum blues, but that term didn't exist at the time. So I suffered alone and ignored my feelings.

The problem was suddenly illuminated one night after a game of bridge with my husband's cousin and his wife. At home, I announced that I was *never ever* going to play bridge again because I hated it. I was furious. My husband told me we would do things his way — besides, everyone else liked to play bridge. Even though I played well and we often won, I didn't like the game. I ran to the bathroom saying, "I would rather die than play bridge again." Then I locked the bathroom door.

It was like a scene from a television show, but this was my life. My husband stood outside the bathroom door, telling me how silly I was. He wanted me to open the door, but I couldn't stop crying. I had not shed a tear in over two years, because my husband did not tolerate tears. He ordered me to stop crying, but the more he talked, the harder I cried. I cried all night long, and begged him to see a counselor with me.

The next morning, my husband took me to a psychiatrist, who talked to me for less than an hour. When I repeated the statement from the previous night — that I would rather kill myself than play bridge — the psychiatrist concluded I was a threat to myself. He convinced me that I needed to be hospitalized. It was the only hope for healing, he said. I was still teary-eyed, tired, and must have looked a mess. Within hours, I was admitted to a mental hospital. There was no chance to go home and say good-bye to my children.

I received seventeen electric shock treatments in a period of six weeks. Mom flew out from North Dakota to care for my children while I was in the hospital. The doctors kept me heavily sedated. At times, I didn't even know my own mother when she came to visit. Shock treatments are traumatic and inhumane.

After the hospital discharged me, I realized the extent of the memory loss that the treatments caused. I knew nothing about my home or the location of my personal things in the house. I had always relied upon — and been a bit proud — of my memory abilities. In order to learn what was in each drawer and cabinet, I cleaned the entire house. Soon after my release, I decided to drive over to a girlfriend's house. Four hours later, I was lost. Formerly salutatorian, head of the class in high school, with the second-highest grades, the loss of my memory was a greater trauma than the treatments. Though I was no longer hospitalized, my psychiatrist kept me so heavily medicated that it was difficult to function. I went to his office for weekly sessions.

Somehow, some way, a miraculous gift came into my hands. It was the book *The Power of Positive Thinking* by Norman Vincent Peale. As I read it, I cried, wishing it could be true that my own positive thoughts could change my life. It couldn't be that easy. After re-reading the book a few times, I decided to experiment. I wanted the lessons to be true; yet I didn't want to build up too much hope just to have it dashed if things didn't work out. After my husband went to work, and the children were outside playing, there was finally time for myself. I set the stove timer for five minutes and spent the time thinking positive thoughts. Soon, my sessions were fifteen minutes long. Finally, I was up to an hour a day of positive thinking. Each time, I felt better. The longer I practiced, the more I healed.

Within a month, I didn't need to set the timer in order to hold positive thoughts in my mind for an hour. Something good was happening to me.

Even though it was only in my mind, I felt better in both mind and body. I wondered: if this works in my house where I feel safe, would it work outside the house? I drove around in the car, working with positive thoughts as the book suggested. I sent blessings to people and found myself feeling stronger and healthier just by deciding to think more positively. I was changing my mind, and my outlook on life was changing. According to statistics, only a small percentage of people who undergo electric shock treatments ever improve their outlook on life. That's why I feel Dr. Peale's book was sent to me by God — to help make changes in my thought processes.

When I left the psychiatric hospital, I made a firm decision never to return to that place or the state of mind that put me there. To this day, I don't know how that little miracle book got into my hands. It was an answer to a prayer that I did not even know I was praying. I shall be eternally grateful to Dr. Norman Vincent Peale for his book, which transformed my life minute by minute. He provided the tools that I needed. At first, I used them in ways that were awkward and unskilled. After many slips and detours, I acquired the ability to be positive more often than before.

I didn't realize the extent of my transformation until the day a former hospital roommate came to visit me. Her state of mind and her actions had not changed. The handwriting was on the wall that she would require hospitalization again. I tried to discuss the power of positive thinking with her, hoping it would help her. She just laughed at me, and the sound gave me goose bumps. She only wanted pills — they made her happy.

The last day that I met with my psychiatrist, I asked him "why" when he asked me a question. He always said, "What do you think?" On my way home from his office, I decided never to see him again. I felt a commitment from the deepest soul level to do whatever was required to change my life. I told my family that the doctor had released me. Financially it was a great relief, and my husband never questioned it.

There were many reasons to stop psychiatric treatment, but one that stands out in my mind is how my daughter was affected. One day, Janine got into my purse and found my tranquilizers. I didn't know if she had swallowed any pills or not! I immediately called the doctor, whose only advice was to keep an eye on her. By that evening, it was clear that Janine was fine, but I flushed all my medication down the toilet, and have not taken a tranquilizer since. Shortly after that event, my former hospital roommate was re-admitted to the hospital.

This self-induced nervous breakdown (also called "baby blues") was the beginning of an awakening. That night after the bridge game, when I started to cry, I could not stop. Crying was not acceptable to my husband. To escape the emotionally repressive situation at home, and to make some decisions, I went into the hospital. At home, my husband's perspective dominated. Everything was black or white, right or wrong. No gray areas were allowed in my life. After I learned the positive thinking process, I used it on this situation. My life was about to change dramatically. The transformation would be directly connected with my willingness to break old patterns in an extreme and physically uncomfortable way.

Even though I was happier and more positive, I still felt empty inside. My husband said feeling empty was not important — I should get on with my life and forget it. Hearing this made me feel terrible. I thought a new house might fill the emptiness. The children were older and needed separate bedrooms. We moved from a little brick bungalow to a new house with four bedrooms. It took a lot of my time to turn this new place into a real home. The distraction helped, but it didn't address the core issue.

Throughout my childbearing years, I had complained to my doctor of different ailments. After years of dismissing my symptoms, my doctor discovered a cyst on one of my ovaries, and recommended surgery. I woke up after surgery and learned that my uterus, both ovaries and part of my bowel had been removed. What a shock! Even though I didn't want more children, the option was always there. My medical problems were extensive — the doctor said it was a wonder that I was able to walk around.

My doctor was more knowledgeable about the effects of nutrition on health than many doctors of those years. He suggested no canned foods and a limited amount of frozen foods. My prescribed diet was fresh fruits and vegetables. After my surgery, the doctor told me my medical problems could have caused the release of toxins. That may have been why I experienced roller coaster emotions after Janine was born. The source of my depression may have been physical, not mental Perhaps the shock treatments were unnecessary. Of course, this was all after the fact. Remember, *not all is good, but good comes from all.*

A few days after surgery, I went home. The doctor was convinced by my red pajamas, freshly brushed teeth, and styled hair that I could leave the hospital early. I arrived home to a great surprise: new carpet in our new home. I was so pleased. On my second day home, with the children at a baby-sitter and my husband at work, I vacuumed the new carpet. Soon I was hemorrhaging.

I drove myself to the doctor's office. He was most upset with me. After he treated me, I drove home thinking of his strict instructions — lay flat and do as little walking as possible. In other words, take it easy. Easy was not a word in my vocabulary, let alone in my life. I was a Type A personality, used to doing everything myself.

I wanted to do something positive with all the idle time, and decided to read the Bible in its entirety. When I was senior in high school, our class studied the Old Testament. After re-reading it, I decided the New Testament had to be easier. I read chapter after chapter, thinking these were nice stories, but I never really understood the heart of them. The mission was accomplished, but I was no more enlightened than before.

If I could have expressed my tears during my

marriage, life would have been a lot different. It was easier to hide my emotions, because that is what my husband wanted. I know now that we were both dealing with control issues. Tears are part of a healing process, a release or even an expression of happiness. But if there is no safe place and time to express the feelings behind the tears, the feelings stay dormant and create problems. Without passing judgment, but aware of the changes in me, I evaluated our marriage. My husband still refused to see a marriage counselor. Ultimately, the changes that occurred in our marriage were my responsibility. He was the same person as always, but I was not.

In reflection, the route that I chose served me. It was the most dramatic way and certainly not easy. This pivotal point in my life changed my thought system and my whole foundation of understanding. I have forgiven the doctor for recommending that I be committed to a psychiatric hospital. I have also forgiven my husband for his inability to accept my tears. My emotional outbursts and its results enabled me to forgive. With this forgiveness, my inner spiritual strength deepened. Reflecting on these things was the beginning of my truth journey.

NOT ALL IS GOOD, BUT
GOOD COMES FROM ALL.

Chapter 7

Starting Awareness

My physical recovery was speedy and complete. I went to work in real estate field and stayed busy selling. Special classes prepared me to take the state exam in order to get my license. The test had two parts, and my scores on both were very high — 97 and 100. I was so excited at my achievement, and I called my instructor to share the good news. He had always made it clear that he expected me to do poorly, so my grades surprised him. He said, "I thought you were cut out to be a social worker and you get the highest grade in the whole class." His exact words are too colorful to quote. Perhaps he sensed on some level that I wouldn't be in the profession for long. I enjoyed the work and social contact offered by this field of work, and I was very successful.

My specialty was selling raw land to homebuilders. I earned a commission and took an exclusive back on the homes, meaning that I listed all the homes built on that piece of property. Part of my job included helping the new homeowner select interior items such carpet, countertops, and light fixtures. Many of my customers and business associates became my friends during this time.

These were in addition to the friends that my husband and I cultivated during our marriage.

During the time when I read *The Power of Positive Thinking,* I also read a newspaper article about someone recalling a former life — a case of reincarnation. The article thrilled me because the idea was so new to me. I called a neighbor and read the article to her. She believed that the article was the work of the devil. My neighbor suggested we work to expose such works, and not read further about reincarnation. I was confused, because part of me wanted to believe in these ideas. Another part of me wondered if she was right. *The Power of Positive Thinking* was opening the door to new avenues for me, and I didn't know where they would lead.

My husband and I socialized with several families in the Seattle area who were former North Dakotans. Our children were within months of being the same ages and we wives used the same gynecologist. The men were all avid hunters. Every fall when hunting season rolled around, we became "hunting widows." From Friday night until Sunday, our husbands were gone. They took camping gear and guns into the mountains to hunt whatever game was in season at that time.

These weekends were not much fun. One of the hunting widows (I'll call her Betty) had three children. Between the two of us, there were five children. We decided to go out for the evening, so we pooled our money and hired a baby-sitter. We did not drink or go to bars, so we wondered what we might like to do. Betty ran a part-time business selling cosmetics, and heard about "table tipping," a monthly event at the home of one of her customers. We left that evening ready to experience the unknown, but with some apprehension. Betty and I made a pact to keep our activities a secret from our husbands.

Upon arriving, we were escorted into a dimly-lit basement where nine or ten people waited. I didn't know any of them. Because we were new, one of the experienced participants explained what was going to happen: The group sat silently around a table with each person's fingertips touching the table. Someone asked "the spirit" to enter the table. When the table moved (indicating the spirit had arrived), people asked the spirit questions, and someone in the group interpreted the answers. The table would tip or tap out different responses, which were written down.

Betty and I sat next to each other at the table. A long, drawn-out process ensued to get answers to the questions. Imagine how it would be if each time you asked a question, the answer was spelled out letter by letter.

After the question was asked, and the table began its response, my mind wandered because I was bored. I soon realized a strange thing was happening. A thought came into my mind, and time after time the table spelled out what I was thinking. This really got my attention! After several hours of this, I told Betty that I knew all the answers before the table answered.

My friend whispered to the person next to her

who whispered to the next person. The group decided to let me answer the questions. Then my answer would be confirmed by the table. I was in a dream-like state and spoke whatever came to me. At first, each person in the group asked a question and I answered it; then the table was asked the same question. The process was lengthy and slow. After a while, we changed the procedure so that I answered questions that were posed to the table.

I said and knew things beyond my scope of knowledge. Some of the questions were very intimate in nature and I gave detailed answers. I advised one person in the group who was having a secret affair at the bank where he worked. I also explained relationships that involved several employees in a company. The group was filled with awe at my answers, but I felt like each person already knew the answer to the question he or she had asked.

One of the couples there asked about their daughter's activities. I gave intimate information about her sexual experiences. Mentally, I traveled to the daughter's room and gave details about the floor covering and placement of the furniture. I advised them to immediately put their daughter on birth control or they would soon be grandparents. The couple denied this, saying that I wrong, and so was the table. They were certain that their daughter was a virgin. Several months later, it turned out that my information was correct, but the parents didn't know it at the time of the message.

If I didn't phrase the answer to the questions

properly, the table communicated that to me by bumping into me. Soon, it became more aggressive. The table pushed against me with such force it almost knocked the wind out of me. The others slid their chairs to follow the movement of the table. At times, I moved out of the way to avoid being hit.

I had an idea that I mentioned to Betty, and she asked the group to let us try it. The other people removed their hands from the table. Then she and I walked around the room, moving the table along with us with just the tips of our fingers. At one point, the table was balanced on one leg, doing a dance like a jig.

This activity lasted until the wee hours of the morning. In a dream-like state of consciousness, I answered questions for hours. The door to the other side was opening for me, but this was my first experience with the non-physical realm. Except for reading *The Power of Positive Thinking,* I was very naive about these matters. The others used words that I had never heard. They felt they had discovered their own personal psychic.

When Betty and I left after two in the morning, we vowed to keep our table tipping experience a secret. The downside of the evening for me was the way I felt the next day. I had a headache the size of a barn, and except for providing the minimal things that the children needed, I was unable to function.

Everyone who attended the table tipping event wanted to get together again. They were very curious to find out if I could communicate with unseen entities again. Another gathering was planned at a different location. Betty and I made sure the event was scheduled for a weekend when our husbands were out of town hunting. We again pooled our money for a baby-sitter. Friends told friends about my performance, and nearly sixty people were expected at the meeting. I was going to be the main attraction.

Since that first event, I had suffered with tremendous headaches. I started to get a headache early in the day prior to the second table tipping event. It kept getting worse. While I prepared for the evening, the pressure made me sick. Many people were present when Betty and I arrived. They treated me like a celebrity. After the table tipping started, I tried to answer questions for several people but nothing came to me. Much to everyone's disappointment, I had to leave the room. I found an empty bedroom, put a damp cloth on my head and fell sleep. Betty and the others continued the evening without me, with the table answering the questions.

On one occasion, a well-known psychic attended. The group was quite large that evening — about thirty people. The psychic gave a short reading to most of the people, and then announced she was done. I approached her, and asked why she had no information for me. She completely ignored me. I was annoyed, but also afraid that she knew something negative, so I made an appointment to see her the next day.

During our appointment, I asked why she

didn't read for me the previous night. She said Spirit told her not to, because I had the same ability that she had. Relying on outside information would prevent me from developing my own ability. She said my mission and life purpose was to live from the Spirit within and lead people to discover their own divine potential. She told me to advise people that all answers are within themselves. With the help of the Inner Christ Presence calling on our angels, everything is at our fingertips. The psychic emphasized that special training would prepare me for my life's work.

This information was exciting! I wanted to tell somebody about these new developments in my life. When I went to the real estate office that week, I told one of my co-workers. He was a fascinating older man named Eb, who was always open to new ideas. He and I could read each other's minds. When I told him about the séance, and about what the psychic told me, he wasn't surprised.

I told him about the classes that I attended on Wednesday nights. The classes included a study group and speakers who specialized in areas of various spiritual belief systems. Topics ranged from speaking in tongues (from the Christian religion) to discussing the purpose of the White Brotherhood. Each person in the class brought a unique perspective of spiritual ideas to the group. The things I learned gave me the understanding I needed to draw a bigger circle — a circle that did not exclude people because of their belief system.

Eb decided to come with me to one of the classes. During class, I realized that this group of people differed from the séance group. There was some discussion about the séance, so Eb and I demonstrated for the group. During the demonstration, I felt the presence of a very strong energy — this experience was more powerful for me than the first one. It was the masculine balance provided by Eb that made the difference. We discovered what our combined abilities could accomplish. When Eb and I were at the table, it followed our fingers. When Eb spoke, I was able to complete the phrase because I knew what he was thinking. People listening said it was like shorthand, because we completed each other's sentences in complete harmony.

NOT ALL IS GOOD, BUT
GOOD COMES FROM ALL.

Chapter 8

Jumping in With Both Feet

My friend Eb continued to attend the Wednesday night classes with me. Neither of our spouses was very supportive. Eb's wife thought we were crazy. My husband said, "Don't bother me with that stuff." They were open enough to agree that we could go together, and that was good enough for me at the time.

Eb and I stopped reading for people. As Spirit shared my life purpose with me, I was directed to develop my spiritual side instead of my psychic side. I was destined to be a bridge-builder, to help individuals connect with the inner God-self. Continuing in the psychic realm would interfere with that. I took the idea of bridge building very seriously. When I told Eb that we shouldn't do readings, he agreed, because he had received the same message. The group was disappointed with our decision. Performing readings had been fun for our egos, but it had to end.

Although my spiritual life was full of new experiences, there were family traditions that continued. My husband and I were very active in adult Sunday School at the Lutheran Church.

Organized religion was important in my adult life, and in my children's lives, because of what I missed in my own upbringing. When I was a child, my parents just dropped me off at Sunday School. They never stayed because it was specifically for children. There was no religious education for adults at that church.

I was born and raised a Lutheran. My grandparents were of Norwegian descent. Later, when my mother started school, she spoke primarily Norwegian. The Lutheran Church was part of my grandparents' heritage. At that time, it held services in Norwegian and English.

My family drove from the country to a small church in a small town in North Dakota to worship. My dad rarely went to church. I am not sure if he believed in God. It became clear to me that he only went when I asked him to. When Dad did attend church with us, we left immediately after the service and missed the social time. To me, going to church meant getting away from the farm and spending time with other young people, so I didn't ask my father to go very often. When I got older, I didn't ask him to go because I wanted to drive the car myself.

When the church needed a teacher for the younger children, they selected me. I enjoyed teaching Sunday school, even though I wasn't formally trained. It was easy for me to mimic what the other teachers did in Sunday school. I especially enjoyed using the flannel board to teach Bible stories to the children. The board was covered with flannel material, and when flannel cutouts were placed on it, they stayed in place. It seemed magical to me. It was so much fun to place the Bible characters upon the board while telling the story of that day's lesson.

When I became a teenager, it was time for confirmation. In the Lutheran Church, that involved studying the Bible, the creeds, and the belief systems of the church. Confirmation students had to do a lot of memorizing and then pass written and oral exams. I was terrified of missing one of the oral exam questions, because the oral exam took place in front of the congregation on a Sunday morning.

The day arrived for our first communion in the church, which included a wafer of bread and Mogen David wine. The minister placed the wafer on my tongue, which was dry from fear, and it stuck on the roof of my mouth. When I drank the wine, I tried to get the wafer loose, but to no avail. For most of the service, I kept trying to produce enough saliva to loosen and swallow the wafer. I don't recall a word of the sermon.

I really liked one particular minister in the church. He and his family became missionaries and were sent to Madagascar, off the coast of Africa. I was intrigued with the idea of doing missionary work, and wondered if I could ever do something like that.

An awakening of sorts happened to me during my senior year of high school. I really felt my faith being examined. My very best friend and classmate had been confirmed with me in the

Lutheran Church. Her mother became very sick. In order for her to continue high school, she had to live with her sister and brother-in-law. They insisted that she become a member of the Seventh Day Adventist church. My friend had no option. All of our fun times of dressing alike and talking about boys ended. She couldn't wear make-up or certain clothes, and she was not allowed to participate in school activities.

I went with her to a special meeting at the Seventh Day Adventist church. During the meeting, other religions were criticized in an attempt to prove that their religion was the only valid one. This scared me. I spoke at length with my own minister about these confusing messages and decided to remain a Lutheran. Just thinking about that meeting evoked feelings of anger and conflict for some time afterwards. My best friend was no longer my best friend. I lost her to religion. Years after we graduated from high school, I visited her and her family in Loveland, Colorado. She still belonged to the Seventh Day Adventist church. It was right for her, but not for me.

My husband never wanted to hear or talk about the spiritual things I learned. I should have realized that the other people at the Lutheran Church would have boundaries on their beliefs, too, but instead it surprised me to discover that they did not embrace what I had to share.

I told the adult Sunday School class that I did not believe in original sin. I believed I could talk directly to God, without needing to go through Jesus. Total silence followed. The minister cleared his throat and proceeded to another topic. The next week, the minister called me into his office. Original sin was one of the tenets of the church. To be a Lutheran, I had to believe it. I didn't. That fateful Sunday morning, I discovered that the Lutheran Church was not a safe place to verbalize what I learned at my Wednesday evening studies. From that day, I took a firm stand to reject those religious tenets.

My husband and I never missed adult Sunday School, children's Sunday School or a Sunday service. My husband coached basketball and softball for the men's teams. We helped build the church physically and financially. It was because of this, I suppose, that the minister said we could continue to lead the teen group — if I agreed never to mention my belief system. The compromise worked for everyone.

My desire to learn about all spiritual matters was unquenchable. I investigated Judaism, White Knights Templar and others, before being led to the Rosicrucian Society. One night a week, I faithfully performed the rituals suggested by the Rosicrucians. At home, I closed the door to my office, to give me privacy for my inner work. No matter how often I asked my family not to interrupt me, they always did. I believe my husband encouraged these interruptions because he wasn't comfortable with what he termed, "Doing witch stuff." The distractions didn't deter me. As I lit candles, studied numerology, palm reading, and a potpourri of other areas, I walked a path to the essence of self — my soul.

The vacant feeling within wasn't going away, and I didn't know how to fill it. I took a year off from the real estate business to be an at-home mother and examine what was going on in my marriage. Money was coming in from my real estate sales, so I contributed to the household expenses. My husband remained adamant that there was no need for us to seek out a marriage counselor. His response was always that WE didn't have a problem. If I had a problem, I should do something about it. So I did.

NOT ALL IS GOOD, BUT
GOOD COMES FROM ALL.

Chapter 9

Listening to God

During this time of self-discovery, I became good friends with a woman named Laurie. Laurie invited me to attend a Sunday service at the Unity Church of Seattle. Although she wasn't a member of Unity, Laurie knew people who attended there regularly, so she was familiar with the basic beliefs of Unity. Laurie felt guided to take me there, and I am eternally grateful that she followed her guidance. I have been in Unity ever since. I was so blessed to have Laurie in my life.

Here are the Unity Spiritual Principles that I learned:

The Nature of God
There is only One Presence and One Power in the Universe, God, The Absolute Good, Omnipotent.

Divinity of Humankind
I am Divine. You are Divine. We are Divine. The presence of God is within me, within you, within all of us. The Christ, individualized in every person, was fully expressed in Jesus, The Christ.

Law of Mind-Action

My thoughts, your thoughts, our thoughts, are connected feelings that are creative and powerful. The Law of Mind-Action states that, "Thoughts held in mind produce after their kind. Whatever I give my attention to unfolds." We create our own experiences with our thoughts and beliefs. We can change our experiences by changing our thoughts! When each of us takes responsibility for our own life, we regain the power previously relinquished to outer conditions and discover the ability to respond in a new way.

Affirmations and Denials

Affirmations and denials are "yes" and "no" statements that affect our minds, thoughts and beliefs. Denials and affirmations change us, not God, and bring us into alignment with the Christ-self, the Higher Self. We are not denying the existence of an actual appearance or event — we are denying that the outer circumstance has power in and of itself. Affirmation is affirming what we want, with the faith that it can manifest, regardless of external appearances.

Prayer, Meditation and the Silence

God is active and present in every person's life. Prayer, Meditation and the Silence are ways that to become receptive to hear the voice of Spirit within. God is divine love. Love is the primary purpose and most important goal of every person. Prayer is talking to God. Meditation is listening to God. The Silence is becoming *one* with God — letting God breathe us as we breathe God.

This was a very intense period of my life, a

time when my spiritual searching was rewarded by amazing discoveries. One night, Laurie and I went to a different church to see a special healing event. These activities were outside my realm of experience, so I was very excited about attending. Laurie and I sat together in the back. Up front was a charismatic nineteen-year-old, who was a great speaker. He invited people to come forward for laying on of hands so they could be healed. I watched this young man lay on hands and speak in tongues. The people he touched seemed to faint, and were then healed. The power in this room was something I had never felt before. I saw miracles with my own eyes, such as people leaving wheelchairs or dropping crutches and walking. My skeptical mind denied what was happening, yet it appeared to be genuine.

Immediately after the service, Laurie and I left. We had plans to attend a jazz concert, but first we wanted to eat. There was a little diner not far from our home, so we stopped there for a sandwich. I remember watching the cook and the waitress going about their ordinary activities: preparing the toast, placing the lettuce leaves, pouring coffee. It was in such contrast to the inspired healings at the church. Physical bodies need energy. Sometimes the energy comes directly from the Source, and sometimes the energy comes to us indirectly, in the form of sandwiches and coffee.

Laurie drove that night. This was the late 1960's, and her Ford Fairlane was almost new. Over the course of ten minutes or so, our bodies were transported from the diner to the club, a dim and crowded room filled with smoke. Tonight the venue was jazz music. It was a popular lounge, and Laurie and I mingled with many of our friends. The band started to play; the sounds of their instruments merged with the smoke and the energy of their efforts became palpable.

It was near midnight when I returned home. I changed my clothes and got into bed. My husband was a heavy sleeper, and rarely woke up when I came in late. This time was different. Not only was he awake, he wanted an explanation because it was so late. I told him about my evening, including the part about the young healer. My husband stopped me. "You don't believe in that stuff, do you?" he asked.

No one had ever asked me that before. I paused, and thought about his question, before I heard myself saying, "Yes, I think I do!" My husband was shocked, but I had strong feelings about these important and personal experiences. "Yes, I do believe that spiritual healing can occur," I repeated, as he continued to question me.

My husband almost yelled his next words: "You cannot believe in that!" It was my turn to be shocked, and I asked him for a reason.

"I forbid you to believe in that," he replied. "I am your husband and you must do what I say."

My head was spinning; I was stunned at his words. I sat up in bed and heard myself say, "You forbid me to do what? Excuse me. If that is the case, we don't have a foundation to continue this marriage. You had better leave this bed and this place right now. We can and will end this marriage."

These words had been hidden in my thoughts, but never before had been spoken. I felt relief that they were finally in the open, relief that his demands pushed me to a decision. Much to my surprise, my husband got out of bed, dressed and left the house. I watched the taillights of his pickup truck driving away, and wondered what would happen next.

NOT ALL IS GOOD, BUT
GOOD COMES FROM ALL.

Chapter 10

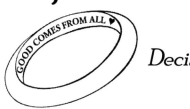

Decision Time —
Divorce

As dramatic as it seemed to watch my husband leave in the middle of the night, this event had been over a year in manifesting. Even though I never spoke forcefully to my husband before that night, I realized as the words came out of my mouth that divorce would lead to our highest good. My husband never moved back into the house.

Two long years of what seemed like insanity followed as our thirteen-year marriage dissolved. My husband tried to convince me to return to the marriage. He encouraged the Lutheran minister and many friends to talk sense into me. When that didn't work, he applied financial pressure and then violence. His violent nature had not been apparent to me — no physical fighting went on between us during our marriage. The only warning I had was during our courtship, when he threatened to harm himself if I ended the relationship. As I reflect on the things that he said and did during our marriage, his violent tendency shouldn't have surprised me, but people typically see only what they want to see. I was no exception.

I arranged for a no-contact court order, which my husband constantly ignored. He tapped my telephone and accused me of sleeping with every man in the area. Once, he held a gun to my head and said if he couldn't have me no one else could either. My reply was evidence of my new faith in spiritual continuity: "Pull the trigger. You can't take my life, only my body."

My husband refused to sign the divorce papers. I spent thousands of dollars on attorneys, and it wasn't enough. When my money ran out, so did their counsel. At that point, I was forced to use legal aide to finalize the divorce. More than my conduct was at stake — my newly-found Unity Church was also on trial. Unity Church was being blamed for our marital problems, for my independence, and for everything!

There was a time that I really feared for my life during the two years. My husband abducted me from the house one night, took me to the mountains, and threatened to drive over a cliff. Yet all was in divine order. I remained silent, and in my heart affirmed that the help of God is always present. During this unbelievable situation, he described in detail a list of accusations against me. Listening, I started to cry.

My husband shouted with glee, "That's exactly what I wanted you to do. With your emotional instability, I will have you committed to the mental hospital again. Then I will be able to control you." Eventually, he drove me home, declaring he would arrange for my commitment the next day. That was purely a scare tactic, which never came to pass.

During this time, most of my friends had restraining orders against my husband. He was obsessed with forcing me to return to married life with him, and his efforts included harassing my friends. The children were involved in the drama, too. They always stayed with a baby-sitter after school. One day, after shopping with a friend, we returned to her house before I went to pick up the children. My husband was parked at the edge of her property when we arrived.

He walked over to my car and started it with a spare set of keys. I ran over and opened the passenger's door. He pulled me into the car and took off. He was ranting and raving about infidelity. If he couldn't have me, nobody would. Then he pulled a gun from a paper bag and threatened me. After driving around for about an hour, I convinced him to take me back to my friend's house to pick up my purse. When he let me out of the car, I went inside and called the police.

I had agreed to meet my husband at the edge of the property and go with him. There was another plan arranged by the police. As I walked toward the pickup, they would stop him and check for a gun permit. The police would then inform him of the restraining order and arrest him.

When my husband saw the police and tried to drive away, the police stopped him. There was, however, no gun in the pickup truck. While I was inside on the telephone, my husband had gotten rid of it. Besides that, my friend's house was located in the city, but the restraining order was issued in the county. The police didn't have the authority to arrest my husband.

By this time, I was late picking up the children. When I arrived at the baby-sitter's house, my children were missing! What an ordeal! I was back on the telephone with the police, and they urged me to find another place to stay that night.

The police discovered that my brother-in-law picked up my children from the baby-sitter's house, and took them home with him. While I went to get them, the officers detained my husband. Picking up my children wasn't a simple matter; I argued with my brother-in-law for some time before he allowed us to leave. During this time, I found out that the missing gun was right there in my brother-in-law's house.

As I drove away with my children, a pickup truck appeared in my rearview mirror. My husband was following us. I lost him after making a series of random turns. *This can't be happening to me, to the children, to us,* I kept thinking. At the house, I grabbed a few clothes for the children, and arranged to stay the night with a friend whose property was covered by the restraining order. We felt safe, at least for one night.

My wonderful friends provided me with a great support system. These male and female friends were my family by choice. My husband couldn't accept the idea of me having friendly relationships with other men. Anytime males were around, my husband showed up at the house, accusing me of having an affair. I would have been a very busy woman to have all those affairs. It seemed odd that he knew every time I had male visitors over. It turned out that the neighbors contacted my husband whenever cars or visitors were at the house.

During this stressful time, which I often thought of as a joke, I did something that wasn't very wise. It was likely that the telephone was tapped, since my husband worked in electronics and knew how to do those kinds of things. Just to agitate him, I made up stories to tell the other person on the telephone. He was stressed from trying to watch me twenty-four hours a day, and ended up having a car accident. Of course, I was blamed for it. Later on, he lost his job because of his obsession with watching me.

Another time, my husband tried to force me back into our marriage by hot wiring and taking my car, so I wouldn't have any transportation. I was working four jobs at the time, and with no way to get to work, I lost them all. Luckily, my children went to school on the bus.

To anyone looking at my situation, it must have seemed critical — there was no cash on hand (less than twenty-four dollars in the bank), no job, two kids, no transportation. Thank God I was in my new way of thinking, and that is when God started to demonstrate miracles in my life.

NOT ALL IS GOOD, BUT
GOOD COMES FROM ALL.

Chapter 11

The Children Leave

It took several months before I was able to support my children and myself. During that time, I had no choice but to use food stamps. For some time, I didn't have a car. With so much conflict taking place all around me, it was more important than ever to fill my thirst for spiritual truth. Because I lived eighteen miles from the Unity Church, my church friends would pick me up for class, bring me home and pay for my baby-sitter. Humans are spiritual beings, but we inhabit the physical world — my friends helped my spirit when they helped meet my family's needs.

One day after the children left for school, I walked into town to buy groceries. I purchased too much to carry, so I called the woman who always gave me a ride to church on Sunday. She drove me home. On my way into the house, I stopped at the mailbox. Inside, there was an envelope from my bank. My first thought was that my account was overdrawn. I opened the envelope and found a deposit slip for $200. When I called the bank to notify them of the mistake, the teller said someone deposited the money into my account. I was amazed, and asked the teller repeatedly who the donor was, but she never told me.

I was always taking classes at Unity Church, and the topic of the current class was prosperity consciousness. Our textbook was *Prosperity, Secret of the Ages* by Catherine Ponder. By the third week of class, I was definitely seeking the loaves and fishes. "This doesn't work," I told the teacher. "I haven't manifested any money." He asked me about my situation, and I said I couldn't support my family even though I worked four jobs (one full-time and three part-time). The teacher said, "Obviously you aren't depending on God for your good or your supply." His answer insulted me, and I decided to leave the class. That same week I lost all of my jobs.

The old was falling away to make way for the new. My first priority was buying a car, which I found in the classified ads. One of my church friends was married to a man who knew a lot about cars. He went with me, so I felt confident about buying something that would run. The price was $150 plus $50 for insurance. My car was a light blue Ford Fairlane with a ripped and sagging headliner, a rusted-out body and bald tires. In the car wash, I needed an umbrella because of all the leaks. Washing the car didn't help much, but I had transportation again — now it was time to look for a job.

The goodness of friends came just when I needed it. Two days after buying my car, a neighbor gave me a job, and I returned to the prosperity classes. Each time I drove my car, I hoped the tires wouldn't go flat, and that it wouldn't rain. Within a couple of weeks, I received a call from a gentleman asking, "When can we put tires on your car?" It sounded like a sales pitch, and I told him I couldn't afford new tires. It took several minutes of explanation for me to understand that I didn't need to buy anything. Apparently, someone had gone into the tire shop, purchased tires for my car, and the shop was waiting to install them for me. God was in action again.

My children thrived on the Unity Church teachings. They especially enjoyed Sunday School. As I became comfortable with the things I learned in my own classes, I shared with them. My children were so good at manifesting. It was easy for them to put into practice what they learned. We often practiced the breath techniques presented in *Little Me and Great Me* by Lou Austin. This children's book describes how to blow out the Little Me when you don't like what is happening, and breathe in the Great Me. My children experienced great success changing their feelings from negative to positive. It was a joy for me to witness them taking responsibility for their own moods and behaviors.

It was already autumn, and as Christmas drew closer, there was no money in reserve to purchase gifts. To earn extra money, I learned how to crochet beaded rings and jewelry. I don't know if it was out of sympathy for my financial state or if people really liked the jewelry, but I sold a lot of it. After one Sunday service, a friend stuck money in my pocket so I could buy Christmas presents for my kids. When I looked in my pocket later, I found $100 — I cried. I could have crocheted until Hell froze over, but never come up with that kind of money. To show my gratitude and share my miraculous abundance, I purchased gifts for a needy family, too. It was a time of multiplying the loaves and fishes. What an awesome feeling to know that $100 went so far!

My husband's possessiveness and jealousy continued. One weekend when the kids were staying with me, he came over unexpectedly while we were eating dinner with one of my male friends. A tirade followed. I wondered how eating dinner with a friend could result in these kinds of accusations. He grabbed the kids and left. Another time, when the children were scheduled to stay with him, my husband asked me to take care of them. One of the neighbors was reporting all my activities to him, and he knew I had overnight guests from out of town.

Our kids were being used to further my husband's plan of keeping me away from my Unity Church friends. It was not always possible for me to take the kids on short notice. Sometimes I was scheduled to work. I refused to cater to my husband's whims, so he accused me of not loving my children. I knew it wasn't fair to our children to be fighting about the when, where or how I was going to spend time with them.

During our marriage, my husband and I hardly ever fought. It seemed like the reason our marriage wasn't working went deeper than just compatibility. We were more like brother and sister than husband and wife. This feeling was confirmed by my spiritual senses. Through dream work and regression sessions, I came to understand the spiritual agreement we made prior to this lifetime. I took my personal reflections and shared them with people who have wisdom gifts and see life patterns.

This is the story.

In my dream, the first pictures that came to me were of me traveling on a ship to the "new world" from England. We sailed through rough waters. I wore a long black dress with a white collar. My hair was pulled back off my face in a severe bun affixed at the nape of my neck. I was unmarried. My brother, his very pregnant wife and his son traveled with me.

During the rough trip, my brother's wife died while giving birth to a daughter. The mother was buried at sea. After a short service, the body was slipped overboard where the waves quickly embraced her. When we arrived at a small port to take on fresh water and supplies, my brother never returned to the ship. He left two children fatherless and motherless because he was uncertain about going to the new world.

Out of a sense of duty, I raised the two children. I was a very stern, aloof woman, the type of woman who did not show love. In this dream, I noticed an interesting thing about those two children. The infant girl had crossed eyes, although the condition didn't show up for a few months. The young boy needed to learn discipline, and the one and only time I boxed his ear, I broke his eardrum, and he became deaf.

Both of my children have experienced the same conditions in their present lives that I saw for my brother's children in this dream. My son David is deaf in one ear because of surgery that was required after recurrent ear infections. My daughter Janine had eye surgery to treat crossed eyes when she was nine months, and again when she was two years old. My children carried this soul memory with them into this lifetime.

In the dream, when we arrived in the New World, I raised my niece and nephew without help. I was very poor, and at times all we had to eat was gruel. This might explain why I am so drawn to money in my present life. The building where we lived was built with our own hands. It was very cold in the winter, and hot in the summer. My hands were cracked and bleeding most of the time from all the hard work and rough weather. I didn't know how to express love in that life, but I did provide a meager existence. After the boy matured, I remember waving good-bye to him as he headed out west. He had a gun over his shoulder, and wore moccasins and buckskin pants. I never saw him again. The girl grew up, married, had her own family, and moved several counties away. I only saw her a few more times in that life.

I experienced my death in that lifetime during a session of past life regression. I was sleeping on straw, and it seemed like I died of consumption. It was freeing to leave my body, because it had been a hard life and I never did learn much about love. Having all this revealed to me explained why my own children primarily lived with their father in this lifetime. It was a karmic tie. Their father needed to complete his karmic responsibility instead of "jumping ship" again.

In a past life, the father had abandoned his children, but in this life he raised them. In this life, I was to love my children but not raise them. This was how events balanced out in this lifetime. It all happened for a purpose. This explained the relationship and the type of love that my husband and I had for each other. Yes, we had problems, but he was and is a wonderful man.

That was not the only past life that I experienced. My husband and I were also married in another lifetime. I gave birth to two souls (my children from this life). I felt an avid need to write about my spiritual journeys, which I did under another name, because it wasn't legal for a woman to write anything in that time period. Someone discovered that I was the author of the spiritual literature. Due to the shame this brought upon the family, my husband divorced me, took the children and left me. I joined a convent, committed myself to a life of introspection and stopped writing. A proud man, my husband never contacted me again and remarried to have a mother for our children. I died in the convent without ever seeing my children again.

Another revelation brought about by the dream and regression work dealt with the root of my attraction to my husband. I was attracted to his charming, pleasant nature. He had all the same characteristics as my grandfather, who I totally loved. But I found out later in my life that Granddad was a dominating and manipulative man who wanted everyone under his control. That was also the hidden nature of my children's father.

I continued my intense studies of the Unity Church teachings as time drew near to the finalization of my divorce. In the interim, I received a letter from my mother calling me a witch. Misperceptions often occur when people observe someone walking a path unlike their own. All the information my mother had was based on what my husband had told her. With that accusing letter from my mother, which my husband had taken from me, we went to court.

When my money ran out, the attorney I hired stopped returning my calls, and I was forced to turn to legal aid. My legal aide didn't do his homework. The letter from my mother was read in court. I had ten people from Unity as character witnesses and a letter from the minister, but the person representing me never introduced the evidence. The character witnesses were not allowed to speak. Documentation of illegal acts by my children's father wasn't presented.

The judge asked me only one question: Did I have any regrets about a relationship I had during my two-year separation? When I said no, he granted custody of the children to their father. The judge's decision was based on that one answer and the fact that I showed no tears or regrets about the divorce.

The children were scheduled to go live with their father in six months. I decided not to delay the changes. It would be easier for the kids if they left right away — then the change would take place at the beginning of the school year instead of six months into it. I remember going home and putting the kids to bed. After the children were asleep, I went into my bedroom, covered my head with a pillow, and cried and cried. I did not want them to hear me, because it was important that they see me accept the new custody arrangements.

Light, Light, Light Everywhere

In the midst of my grief and desolation, I was suddenly aware the room was flooded with light. The light was so pure and white that I thought someone had turned the light on in the bedroom. When I took the pillow off my face, the room was filled with the Spirit of Light. I was filled with great apprehension at this unknown wonder. Then I felt a deep caress of love wash over me. I sensed rather than heard a gentle voice. I felt it was Jesus Christ as I imagined He would be. This presence said, "My child, let's go for a walk." The light grew brighter and brighter as this Presence led me to a garden where we walked. "Do not despair. This is something you agreed to before you were born."

The Light Presence spoke again: "You were offered the choice of giving birth to these children and you agreed to that. For your children's father to have a purpose in life, he must raise them from this point on. Clarity will be given to you. You have millions of children to feed with Truth."

The Christ Presence showed me my extended family, with groups of them all over the world. I was told they were my children. I would prepare to be with these extended children while my birth children would be raised by their father as agreed before birth. This pact felt like a great purpose for this lifetime. The garden that we walked in was beautiful, both physically and spiritually. I was assured that the Presence of Light would be with me always, and I would never be alone. All was well, even though I didn't or couldn't see the whole picture at that time. "My peace is yours," this Presence said. "All of this is for a purpose."

It was like time stood still. Slowly, I felt myself returning to the bedroom, where I opened my eyes. The room was dark, but the sweet Presence was there. I believe Jesus Christ appeared to me in a structure I could understand. Since that time, I have a deeper understanding of the spiritual essence of all Master Teachers. I have communed, communicated, and directly experienced Mother Mary, the Buddha and other Masters. But the most profound was that first time, experiencing the energy of Jesus Christ. It was such a sweet, sweet moment that my tears of grief turned into tears of gratitude. My children chose to come through my body, and we had chosen each other, agreeing to face these circumstances together.

I went to the children's room. They stirred in their sleep, but didn't wake up. I kissed them both and told them how much I loved them. I said that I would miss them very much, but their father was a wonderful man who would take care of them. It was easier to release my children to their biological father now that I knew their Heavenly Father was in charge.

During my separation, and until the judge's ruling, it never occurred to me that I would be denied custody of the children. It came as a total surprise as well to my Unity friends (who were in court with me), my minister, and even to my family. I was a great mother for the children. When it came time to fulfill my contract and commitment to them, I was not prepared for the way it unfolded, but because of the vision, I had peace of mind. There was a reason we had to part — a reason that could be perceived by the spirit, but not the everyday mind.

The next morning, it was time to get the children ready to leave with their father. I tried to make a festive occasion out of the whole event, emphasizing how much fun we would have when they came to visit. David and Janine were ready to go when their father arrived. They were laughing, excited, and in a fun and playful mood. This caught my former husband off guard. He viewed this event as a victory, but he wasn't really prepared to take custody of the children. It was going to be an adjustment for him, too. His words to Janine and David as they left were, "Come on kids, your mother doesn't want you, so I will take you with me and we will move away from here."

The children looked confused. I waved farewell and yelled, "Remember, I love you!" To this day, tears flow freely when I recall that time, doing the hardest thing I had ever done. In this life, I knew I had to let my children go, and trust that the guidance from my vision was correct. Although my human heart wanted them with me, my spirit heart saw the bigger picture. I was lifted up to a higher understanding because the energy of the Presence was still with me.

My ex-husband lived in North Dakota. He took the children there, and remarried within the year. His new wife was the woman who baby-sat the children during our separation. She had one son from a previous marriage.

Several years later, my ex-husband spent a year in prison on false charges. His wife and my children proclaimed his innocence, but the court believed the accusations of a troubled child.

Money was scarce, and because my children now lived in another state, I couldn't make the legal arrangements needed to take custody of them. My children lived with their father's sister that year.

Less than two years after my ex-husband's release, the same accusations were made. His wife was given a choice by the court — give up her son, or give up her husband. She chose to give up her son. I know this was all part of a divine plan. Shortly after this happened, my children moved back into the state of Washington with their father and his wife.

My ex-husband had turned into a wonderful parent. I wrote a letter to him and his wife, complimenting them on their involvement with the children. They all went camping and horseback riding together. David joined Civil Air Patrol. Their father attended all their school functions and was a one hundred percent dad. Later, I learned that my children read the letter. After all the fighting and problems between their father and me, they came to understand that we both loved them. Through this process, I became friends with my former husband.

My one regret about the children living with their father was that they couldn't attend a Unity Sunday School. Before the divorce, I remember taking them to church one time when the Sunday School lesson involved teaching the kids to dissolve clouds. They learned quickly, and it didn't take them any time at all to create a blue sky.

Reflection

I now have a clear insight regarding the power of the spoken word. I always said I didn't want children, and the result was that I had trouble conceiving. Even though I spent many hours caring for my younger brothers and sisters — watching, feeding and burping them — it wasn't much fun for me. By the power of spoken words, people connect with their purpose in life. I gave birth to a

son and daughter who went to live
with their father after our divorce.
The pattern of my own desires
created the circumstances so that
there were no children in my life. The
desire for *no children* was a strong
affirmation. The power of the spoken
word was demonstrated for me.

NOT ALL IS GOOD, BUT
GOOD COMES FROM ALL.

Chapter 12

Starting a New Life

It was a grief-filled time for me after my children moved to another state. I often cried for no reason — except that I missed them tremendously. As I endured those sorrowful days, I reminded myself that my children had their own lives to live and experiences to go through. They had chosen their own path.

Money has always been a big issue in my life. I have created that reality. With my need to be prosperous, I felt ashamed to use food stamps. When money was scarce, I used creative tactics to get what I needed. In order to have my hair cut and styled, I would either go without food or trade something. One of my favorite beauticians became good friends with me, and we traded services of different kinds every week. I had a deep commitment to maintain an outer image as well as an inner connection with God and my inner beauty. Basically, I love to look good. At the Goodwill store, I found dresses that would have cost hundreds of dollars for five dollars or less. No one guessed how poor I was. I wore my finest clothes to buy groceries in the early morning when only a few people would see me. It was important to look great when I used my food stamps.

When I had custody of my children, I was entitled to food stamps. Now that they were gone, I didn't feel right accepting that assistance, so I tried to return them. The staff at the government office were baffled. I insisted on giving the food stamps back. They may have destroyed the stamps, as there was no system to deal with returns.

I learned many Truth principles in the beginning of my spiritual journey, and I recall one of my first lessons vividly. One day, I walked into the house and found bags and bags of groceries all over my kitchen. It was overwhelming. When my girlfriend called, I talked to her about not wanting to accept charity. My girlfriend spoke these words of wisdom. "Isn't it time you accepted gifts from someone else? You have given all your life, and you've never allowed yourself the joy of receiving. So in your selfishness of not receiving, you are depriving other people of the joy of giving."

I listened to my friend, and realized I wasn't being very grateful. My pride was hurt, knowing that someone perceived me as too poor to put food on the table. It is an interesting coincidence that I was using the very last of the food in the house on that day. Later, I learned that my brother opened the door for my donor, and he told me who it was. I purchased a rose and took it to her. This woman had helped me on several occasions. The lesson I learned was that you must receive as well as give.

I barely made enough money to pay my bills, even though I worked as many hours as my employer allowed. I couldn't afford to return to the real estate business because even if I sold a house the very first day, I wouldn't receive the money until closing, which could be months later. Some people I knew owned a restaurant with a bar, and I volunteered there a few times. They gave me a part-time position. I had never been a waitress, and didn't know one drink from another, but I was ready to learn. One of the bartenders helped me, and I practiced making drinks. The tips weren't great, but that was because of my honest approach. I didn't mind flirting casually with the male customers, but I made it clear to them that nothing else would happen.

That year, hot pants were a fashion fad. My uniform consisted of white hot pants, a black turtleneck sweater and white boots — not exactly my style! One of my brothers visited me at the bar, and exclaimed, "I can't believe my sister is doing this!"

I needed more money. I heard about an exclusive restaurant opening in Renton (a town near Seattle) which served gourmet food. I continued to work at night for my friends, but during the day I worked in Renton. Unlike my hot pants costume, the uniforms at the Renton club were knee-length starched peach dresses. Service was expected to be very formal and polished. Balancing the food on a tray was a feat for someone who doesn't even cook, but I learned quickly.

It wasn't long before they offered me another shift at dinner, and I accepted immediately. So

93

much for hot pants. The customers during the luncheon shift were primarily businessmen, who were great tippers. The evening guests were mostly families.

The club provided Big Band music on Thursdays, Fridays and Sundays. One day, I was offered a position as the assistant manager. The bartender had been promoted to manager, and he interviewed me. He said, "I have been watching you with all the customers. You're always positive, and you instruct the waitresses when they have problems. You seem to get along with everybody, and I want you to join our team."

It certainly meant more money for me, so I accepted. Two weeks later, my new manager got sick. Who had to do the hiring and training of the waitresses and the musicians? Right, me! This was on-the-job, trial-by-fire learning for me.

The restaurant and the bar opened at seven in the morning. Sometimes I tended bar. I tried to discourage the customers from drinking liquor in the morning, but they told me to mind my own business. One of them commented, "You are either going to sell spirits or save souls." My job was a way to get a paycheck, but there were definite conflicts with my values.

My new life was taking shape. I befriended an aged gentleman, or perhaps it was he who befriended me. I met Hans when I worked as a waitress near one of Seattle's fishing areas. He loved coffee and always tipped me at least a dollar, even though his only income was social security.

Hans rode a bus in order to get to the restaurant. He wanted to spend time near the harbor, and he wanted to see me.

Hans must have been close to ninety years old, with wrinkled skin and pure white hair. He was Norwegian, and in his younger days made a living as a fisherman in Alaska. Cold water fishing is very dangerous, but Hans had loved the work and the freedom of being on the sea. He had many stories to share, and I enjoyed being with him and hearing about his life.

He needed a lot of help with his daily life, and I ended up doing quite a bit for him. Hans had trouble hearing and his eyesight was poor. On Sunday mornings, I drove downtown to the old hotel where Hans lived and we went to Unity Church together. I helped him find a seat in the front row so he could hear and see the service better. He always wore a tie to church, but sometimes it was dirty or had holes in it. Hans couldn't see well enough to know if his clothes had food stains on them — they usually did, since it was difficult for Hans to feed himself. He also smoked a pipe, and every piece of clothing he owned had a hole burned in it. I routinely threw out his soiled clothes and bought him new ones from the thrift shop.

People assumed Hans was my grandfather. Because of his age and the assorted physical challenges he had, some of my friends felt uncomfortable when Hans was around. To me, Hans was family, and I wanted to include him in my activities. One time, I was invited to be the guest of honor at a dinner party. The people hosting the party asked me not to bring Hans. I told them if Hans wasn't invited, I wouldn't be there either.

Things didn't work out very well on the day of the party. It was quite a special occasion, so I wanted Hans and his clothes to be really clean. We went to pick up his suit from the dry cleaners. The dry cleaner was closed; not just closed, but foreclosed! We finally retrieved the suit, but Hans still needed a bath so we arrived late for dinner.

There were a few people who appreciated Hans. Sometimes I took him over to my brother's house. My brother helped him shower. My brother's children loved Hans, and when he came over, they happily jumped all over him. My own children felt the same way.

Hans had a fisherman's spirit, and yearned for the wilderness and its freedom, but his aging body needed constant care. After I finished my seminary work, I was assigned to a Unity Church in California. Hans refused to come to California with me — he wanted to live in Seattle, near the water and the ships. It wasn't long before his condition deteriorated, and I made arrangements for Hans to move into a nursing home. Because he was such a lover of freedom, Hans died within two weeks after being admitted.

I flew back to Seattle for his funeral service. My brother picked me up at the airport and brought one of his sons with him. When my nephew heard the word cremation he wanted to know what that meant. "Aunt Thelma, why are you burning Hans?" he asked.

This turned into an opportunity to share with my nephew that life continues after death. I told him, "It's like clothes — you wash them, outgrow them, and sometimes throw them away. So it was with Hans' outer garment, his body. Hans exists outside of his clothes, and it doesn't matter what happens to his clothes. That outer garment is the only thing that was changed through cremation. Hans' spirit is still alive, but is invisible." My nephew seemed satisfied with my answer.

There were a handful of people at the memorial service, which I led at Unity Church. Hans' ashes rested in a container on a countertop at my brother's house until I took them to Unity Village, where they were scattered in the rose garden.

I know that Hans and I were connected in another life. Hans gave me unconditional support and love. If we were out having dinner and a good-looking man walked by, Hans would point him out and try to step out of the picture. Hans supported me in every aspect of my life. I believe he had the ability to see the future. "You would never believe what I see for you," he often said to me.

The terms of my divorce gave me two years to sell our house and share the profits with my ex-husband. Because of my real estate experience, I opted to sell the house myself. I waited for Spirit to tell me when to advertise, and chose the Fourth of July weekend. Holiday weekends are usually not the best times to advertise, but someone came to look at the house that day and they bought it. Holy Spirit is always on time.

When I went to the bank after closing, I was shocked to learn there was a second mortgage on the house, which my ex-husband used to pay his attorney fees. And I lost custody of my children because I had to use legal aid! I never signed for that loan, but there was a signature above my printed name on the papers. After paying the closing costs and both mortgages there was little money left. I suppose I could have sued my ex, but where would the money for attorney fees come from?

Stuck in a classic Catch-22 situation, I tried to explain things to the mortgage company. They wouldn't do anything, so it was time to be creative. I typed up a document stating that my ex-husband was responsible for the balance of the second mortgage, and it would be deducted from his half of the sales profit. The loan officer said no one in his right mind would sign that.

Probably not, but my ex-husband didn't bother to read the documents that I asked him to sign. When he received the small check, he was not a happy camper. It didn't matter. Because of the circumstances involved with the second mortgage, I knew he wouldn't take any action against me. Except for the children, the house was our last tie. It was time to move on.

NOT ALL IS GOOD, BUT
GOOD COMES FROM ALL.

Chapter 13

The Path

I kept my job at the club in Renton for several years. It was a members-only fraternal club. Female guests were allowed in the restaurant, but not in the bar. As a woman in this environment, I earned a certain amount of respect. I could stop bar fights better than most men. The gal I replaced had been raped in the parking lot after work one night. My brother asked if I was afraid. I replied, "No, you know how flat-chested I am. I would need a tattoo saying 'this side up, in case of rape.'"

My brother thought this exchange was funny and repeated it at a family gathering. In my family, everyone tries to out-do each other when it comes to stories. My brother picked an unlikely time, though — the family was at our grandfather's funeral when my brother said, "Thel, don't you want to tell them about your tattoo?" That got everyone's attention.

I laughed it off and went into the kitchen. My mother followed me, practically on my heels. "You didn't really get a tattoo! How dare you!"

I wanted to reassure her, but at the same time,

99

it was fun to bait her: "Mother, I didn't get a tattoo… yet." Those words have followed me all my life. Even today, people who know this story ask to see my tattoo. That would not be my last encounter with a tattoo anecdote.

My new experiences as a single woman and my spiritual studies at Unity Church were changing my life. A cruise was planned for church members, and I was one of thirty people who paid $1000 to go. I was really looking forward to the trip. The ship would travel south from a California port along the coast and continue down the coast of Central America. Presentations based on the writings of Joel Goldsmith were scheduled for every day of the cruise. His work was known as "The Infinite Way." The trip was going to be much more than a vacation — it was going to be a spiritual retreat.

Shortly before the departure date, the management at the club said they wouldn't allow me to take the time off. So I told my boss, "Consider this my two weeks notice. I made arrangements far enough in advance for you to find someone to cover for me. I no longer work here." That was one of the first things I did for myself.

My plan was to go on the cruise and then stay in California for another week. Even though I was unemployed, I had a fantastic time. The Unity minister told the whole congregation when we returned that I had more fun than anyone else on the ship.

My roommate, like me, was a metaphysical truth student. She gave me my very first metaphysical book *The Game of Life and How to Play It* by Florence Scovel Shinn. My roommate had red hair and was physically well-endowed. She loved life and had an infectious laugh. People in our lives all teach us something: she wanted to be less buxom, and I wanted to be more so.

Our group had an area reserved on the ship for the Unity Truth presentations. There was time to study and discuss the ideas. The people in the group got to know one another and had fun in the process.

There was a shocking opportunity during the cruise for the group to apply the principles that we were learning. The weather was terrible that day — there was a storm and strong winds, and passengers were required to stay off the deck. During the Unity presentation, a loud horn sounded. Then came the astounding message over the loudspeaker: "Man overboard!" While in the process of attaching canvas flaps to protect the passengers, a member of the crew had fallen off the ship. There was no sign of him in the water.

The Unity minister said, "This is the time to do our work." He led us in prayer. "Anytime you think of this man, circle him in white light and say all is well. God is protecting him now."

In a life and death situation, how do you know when you've done all that can be done? It was something I never had occasion to think about before, but people who make their living on ships do think about it. If someone on the ship falls overboard, the ship is required to circle the area for a set number of hours before proceeding. The cruise ship followed this search-and-rescue procedure in an effort to recover the crewman, but without success. Everyone on the ship donated to a fund for the missing crewman's wife and children. The donations amounted to several thousand dollars.

Even though the crewman wasn't found, the minister said to us, "You don't know that he is gone. Always believe he is in the white light and safe." There was no more anyone could do. The ship was less than halfway into the trip, and we continued on.

A year later, on another ship, the church's cruise coordinator overheard a conversation: "This is where we picked up that man last year in shark-infested waters."

The crewman who fell overboard was saved! Our prayers worked, although we didn't know it at that time. Sometimes we never know that our prayers are answered. Once you stay off the ways and means committee, you allow God's work to be done, and God always says, "Yes."

After my vacation was over, I had to face the reality of no job and no money. What was I going to do? The managers at the men's club wanted me to come back to work, but during the cruise, I made a commitment to myself that I would not work nights. I wanted to attend night classes at Unity. The restaurant business was demanding, and there had to be an easier way.

There wasn't enough money for my car payment and rent, but somehow things worked out. One night, a friend invited me to play bingo with her. That night, I won enough money to make my car payment.

A similar thing happened when my children lived with me. They needed school supplies. I thought, "How am I going to do this?" My intuition directed me to the racetrack, although I had never been to a horse race. I started with twenty dollars and made four hundred and twenty. After three days of betting at the track, I won enough money to buy everything the children needed. My purpose was served, and I have never been back to the racetrack again. Spirit used that avenue of supply for my children. God is my Source — it is the avenue that varies.

At the insistence of an employment counselor, I went on an interview at a health food store. Back then, I couldn't tell a vitamin from an aspirin tablet. I smoked, and my diet consisted mainly of soda and candy bars. When I saw the store, it was obvious that the place wasn't making a profit. Surely they wouldn't offer me a job. But there was my voice saying, "Oh, I can start on Monday." What did I get myself into? Then the owner told me smoking was not allowed in the store. I agreed, and never smoked another cigarette after that.

I devoured all the reading material in the store. By the end of the first week I was already suggesting changes. I asked for a commission on monthly sales over $10,000. The owners quickly agreed. Although the store had never sold that much, I earned a bonus the very first month.

About that time, my employer told me that he and his wife were traveling to the Philippines to visit a psychic surgeon. Psychic surgery uses the mind to produce healings for the physical body. It apparently involves separating the magnetic connection which holds cells together.

Left in charge for a month, I redecorated and rearranged the whole store. I served health food samples to the customers, and then started a home delivery service. The owners were in awe when they returned.

While my employer was in the Philippines, he acquired the power to heal. The retail environment at the health food store gave him the opportunity to help many people. When someone with healing needs entered the store, the owner's hands would start to burn. The sensation continued until he laid his hands on the person. Some people were healed with a quick touch, so my employer didn't even need to mention his ability. There were others, with more serious conditions, that he took in the back. In private, he explained his healing ability and asked to help them. The people who accepted his offer received an amazing gift. This man never went to church and didn't consider himself a man of God, but he was completely in touch with the power of the spirit.

About a year later, the owner offered to sell me the store and provide financing. It sounded like a win/win situation for both of us. Just before we were ready to finalize the sale, I had a dream that guided me away from that future. In my dream, the business stayed in the family, taken over by the owner's son. Although the son had never shown interest in the family business, he changed his mind after I talked to him. To this day, he still owns the store.

At the health food store, I learned how to eat correctly and use nutritional supplements. I learned about fasting and cleansing the body. And finally, I helped a family business to stay in the family.

NOT ALL IS GOOD, BUT
GOOD COMES FROM ALL.

Chapter 14

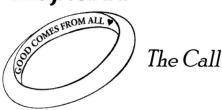

The Call

After leaving the health food store, I started working for a large Alaskan fish company located in Seattle. This company had offered me a job previously, so they were glad to finally hire me. My position was in the accounting department, and it paid more than I had ever made in my life.

One Sunday, the minister at Unity Church asked me about my own plans to become a minister. What plans? At that time, I felt no such aspirations, so I replied, "Never, not me. Who would want to do that?"

In my mind, that was the final word on the topic, but my minister was convinced otherwise. He asked me the same question many times over the next few months. One Wednesday night, we met for dinner before class at one of my favorite restaurants. "You know you are right for this calling," my minister said.

One day, simply to placate him, I agreed to let my minister submit my name to Unity Headquarters for an interview. Within a few days, I found myself meeting with the Dean of Seminary from Unity Village. I apologized to the Dean for taking his time, and said, "It's not the right time for me. I have to decide if I am moving toward a new life or if I am just trying to escape from my old life."

We were having dinner together another time just before the Dean came to town, and my minister asked if I had scheduled an interview. He was becoming a nag!

"For the first time in my life, I have a job that pays well," I said. "Why do you keep asking me to give that up? Please don't push me — I will make my own decisions."

NOT ALL IS GOOD, BUT
GOOD COMES FROM ALL.

Chapter 15

The Dream Message

Just before the Dean of Unity Seminary came to town, I dreamed I was a minister, giving a sermon in front of a congregation. I also dreamed of a meeting with the Dean of Education. We were talking about events that happened when he was a young man.

Even as I dreamed, I knew it was important to remember the details of that conversation and mention them to the Dean. I would later learn that only the Dean and his mother knew of these events. Sharing these dream insights with the Dean helped me get accepted into ministerial school.

When I awoke in the morning, I called for an interview appointment. The guidance was clear — it was time for me to pursue a ministry career.

I was dating a man who also wanted to be a Unity minister. His interview had been scheduled months in advance, so I didn't mention my appointment to him.

It was a surprise to find out that the interview

process included a test to check my knowledge about the history of Unity Church. The test contained questions about the co-founders of Unity and their writings. I had taken many spiritually-oriented classes during the time I attended Unity, but none of them included the history of the church. I didn't even know who the founders were, but it was a little late to turn back. Before the test, I had a chance for some privacy in a waiting room. I did intense prayer work, visualizing the church founders as an extension of myself. If the founders were a part of me, I would know the answers to the test questions.

The test was graded while I waited. When I was called in to meet with the interview team, I found out that I aced the test.

The interview committee headed back to Unity School to determine who would be admitted. I didn't realize there were hundreds of people who applied, and the committee selected just thirty-five of them.

The man I was dating received an acceptance letter. He called me at work to tell me the exciting news. I asked him to open my mail and read the decision to me. What he read had been predicted years ago by my friend Hans — I was accepted into the Unity School of Christianity for the 1974 class.

No one in my family knew about this. I was afraid to tell my mother. During my divorce, she was the one who wrote the letter criticizing my spiritual path and claiming that I was a witch. At that time, the only things my mother knew about

Unity Church were things that my former husband told her. Since then, Mom had only been to Unity once when my brother got married. It was the day before Easter, and the whole family stayed at my place. The next day, we all went to Unity Church together.

When we returned to my house, I fed thirty-five people for Easter dinner. Did I dare ask what they thought of the service? Finally, my mom broke the silence and said, "If I lived closer, I would join that church."

Even though my mother had enjoyed that one service, I still dreaded the thought of telling her about my acceptance to Unity seminary school. The night before my phone was disconnected, I knew it was now or never. I began the call by asking Mom if she was sitting down, because I had something to tell her. Then I told her my plans. There was complete silence — I realized I wasn't breathing. Finally, Mom spoke.

"No one knows what I am going to tell you," she said. "Every time one of my sons was born, I thought about how great it would be to have him become a minister. I never thought it would be my daughter. I'm very proud of your decision."

Mom's words came as a complete shock, and through my tears, I thanked her. I wished that her change of heart concerning Unity had come sooner. She didn't have any idea that the children were living with their father because of her letter.

On my way to Seminary School, I visited my

grandmother, who was very ill and in the hospital. For most of the visit, I sat quietly with her, helping to hold her soul in the light. I also talked softly to her, and told her how loved she was. Grandma was not lucid when I arrived. A few days later, she was alert and enjoyed some great time together with family members. Her condition improved so much that the hospital decided to release her. The day before her scheduled release, Grandma passed away.

After hearing the news, I went to the Peace Chapel at Unity Village to pray for her. I felt like my job was completed, because I had the chance to see her before I entered Seminary. She graduated from the physical dimension that night feeling great and loved by her family. Isn't that a wonderful way to leave your body? Everything works out.

NOT ALL IS GOOD, BUT
GOOD COMES FROM ALL.

Chapter 16

My Spiritual Home

A few weeks before I left Seattle for Seminary School, I visited my doctor for a physical. I didn't want to use another doctor during my two years at school, so my doctor ran a thorough panel of tests. I was rushing around, preparing for my move, when I received a call. My doctor wanted me to come back for a biopsy because my checkup was suspicious.

The biopsy results confirmed the Big "C" — I had cancer. The doctor suggested immediate surgery. I did not have time for this! Inside, I was thinking, "Why now, Lord? Now that I know my purpose, why is this happening to me?"

One day soon after that, I walked into the health food store. It had been weeks since I'd last seen the owner. He told me his hands were burning. When I told him about my biopsy being cancerous, he took me in the back room, prayed and laid hands on me.

Other friends wanted to help, too. I made arrangements with three people to meditate with me for the blessing of healing. Distance does not affect healing, so we didn't need to physically be together in order to pray together.

At the scheduled time, I sat in down in a dark room to meditate. I was not making prayers of petition. Instead, I was just being receptive to goodness and giving thanks for my healing. Suddenly, I felt an intense heat and light, which radiated throughout the whole room, but focused on my body. It was somewhat uncomfortable to experience. When I opened my eyes, the room was still dark. I closed my eyes again, and the light got more intense. The intense heat pulsed through my body in waves. Throughout my entire body, I experienced the certainty of a magical healing that night.

Later that week, I saw the doctor again. He examined me just briefly before he said, "Something has happened. There is a dramatic change in your body where the cancer cells were. But I cannot give you a clean bill of health yet."

Another biopsy came back showing suspicious cells, but the lab results didn't matter to me. Because of my experience that night, I knew unconditionally that my healing was complete. I was healed in spite of what appearances indicated.

Before I ever knew about the cancer, I had listened to some audiotapes on the subject of self-healing. The tapes featured an Air Force officer named Dr. Carl Simonton, who talked about his research with people who had cancer. Dr. Simonton explained how they used imagination, visualization, and inner power to accept the perfection of their bodies. He took slides of his patients before and after the self-healing. While the "before" slides were often gruesome, the "after" slides showed wholeness and perfection. When I listened to the tapes, I didn't realize how pertinent the information was going to be for me.

My doctor released me from treatment, but insisted that I see another doctor immediately after my move. When I went to a doctor in Kansas City, I explained to him that my condition had changed dramatically. I signed a release so my new doctor could obtain my records.

Since the night of my healing experience, I made a regular practice of visualizing my body whole, well, and in a state of perfection. Sometimes I used a children's medical book, and looked at pictures to help me with visualization. Dr. Carl Simonton's tapes were hard to understand because they were old and the sound quality was poor. He had not yet published his book, in which he explained how the power of imagination aided in self-healing.

I visualized every day for an hour before school and again at night, speaking the words of healing in the first, second and third person. I visualized that my healing was completed when my friend from the health food store laid on his hands. I used these phrases:

I, Thelma, am whole and perfect.
You, Thelma, are whole and perfect.
She, Thelma, is whole and perfect.

115

My healing was completed in the spiritual and mental realms on the night when I witnessed the light and radiance of God, but the physical realm sometimes lags behind. I continued my practice with the idea in my mind that the doctor would say, "There is nothing wrong with you. Everything is fine." I always imagined that same message. During meditation, I imagined that I overheard people talking about how vibrant and alive I was. The visualization took on an energy of its own, and contained something to involve all five of my senses. The white light of protection was my mainstay and my comfort, a blanket surrounding me at all times during my sessions.

No one knew about my condition. I didn't tell anyone at school because I thought if they knew about the cancer I wouldn't be allowed into Seminary. I didn't tell my family because I didn't want my mother to worry. I didn't even tell my close friends — I just asked them to hold me in their prayers for health and wholeness.

My medical records were lost in the mail, so months passed before I saw the Kansas City doctor again. He examined me and sent a biopsy for evaluation. At the follow-up visit, the doctor said he had received the wrong file. When I asked him what he meant, he replied, "There is nothing wrong with you. Your biopsy is clear."

It was definitely my file. My records were quite distinctive. It took medical assistance for me to become pregnant the first time, and the same doctor delivered both of my children.

The doctor's declaration perfectly matched my visualization. In order to hold this healing in sacred space, I never talked about it. It was nine months since the night that I experienced being healed. My healing was completed in my mental, emotional and spiritual body, but it took time to manifest in my physical body.

Eventually, I did tell my story. During seminary, each student had the opportunity to arrange and lead an entire service. When it was my turn, I decided to share my healing experience with my classmates, faculty and visitors. The name of my talk and the featured song was "He Touched Me." Sharing my story was awesome, it was scary, and it was a blessing.

I continue to use techniques that engage all my senses in order to demonstrate my hopes, dreams and desires. In fact, that is how this book — once just an idea — came to be a reality.

There is nothing too trivial or too grand for these methods. You can use them to achieve whatever your heart desires. They are tools for living life consciously. To be consciously connected with the universal power does not change it, but this connection changes us and our perception of circumstances. Whatever the challenge, you can heal it, rise above it, or change the situation to create a positive outcome. Concentrate on what you do want in place of focusing on what you don't want. This is one of the basic spiritual lessons that creates a foundation for a miraculous life.

Here are the four steps for you to manifest and

demonstrate your hopes, dreams, and desires. Remember: not all seems to be good; however, good comes from all.

The first step is to **know** what you don't want.

Contrast is very powerful. When you know what you don't want, you are free to ask yourself what you DO want. Too often, we focus on what we don't want and wonder why life doesn't get any better. The more you resist what you don't want, the more you get what you don't want. It is like handcuffing that negative energy to you. With that mindset, you continue to experience what you don't want. Determine what it is you don't want, and then move your thoughts elsewhere.

The second step is to know what you **do** want.

When you ask somebody that question usually they flip back into what they don't want. Instead of thinking, "I don't want to be sick," change the wording of your thoughts: "I want to be well." Take the time to discover what you want. Even though this process seems trivial, it is not always easy to put into practice.

You become a vibrational match to what you want. When you change your vibration, the universal staff works on your behalf. A fascinating thing begins to happen. Withdrawing focus from the things you don't want causes them to wither and be released from your experience. Let go. Achieve a vibration with the universe that reflects what you **do** want.

The third step is to use your power of imagination as a scissors to mentally cut out the physical manifestations of what you want. What would your actions, thoughts and verbalizations be if you already had what you want? In your mind, use self-talk to chatter about it. Experience what it feels like, smells like, and sounds like to achieve your hopes, dreams and desires. Practice this over and over and over again.

The fourth step is to give thanks while you are listening to your inner self. You may want to heal your body or attract a partner into your life. This is a great beginning for you.

Within step three, the tool that you use to become a co-creator with God is the power of the affirmation. The words that you choose for the affirmations will vary, depending on whether you are primarily visual, auditory, or kinesthetic (feeling). This is explained in depth in another chapter. Affirmations are statements that present the truth about what you want. Be sure to affirm what you do want rather than what you don't want. As you affirm what you do want, you become a vibrational match and a mighty magnet of energy to manifest it. An affirmation is more powerful if you make the statement in the first, second and third person. If you work with only one of these, use first person.

To create my own healing, I started with first person to visualize perfect tissue functioning in a wonderful way.

"I am whole and free and vibrantly alive."

In the second person I visualized the doctor telling me, "There is nothing wrong with you. You are whole."

Using the third person, I heard the doctor say to the nurse. "There is nothing wrong with her. She is healed. I don't see anything that would indicate that further treatment is desirable."

When I went to the doctor in Kansas City, his words were almost identical to my visualizations. The only thing he added was, "Let's take a biopsy of the tissue. Even though I can't see anything, let's have it confirmed." I knew the biopsy would support my visualization of the inner movie that took place over the course of nine months.

With a slight variation, the affirmation theme is very powerful to clear blockages in your life. Use this process to create a vacuum, cleanse, and release all blockages within. Begin by choosing an affirmation or statement of truth. Don't rely on facts as they appear, because that does not serve your spiritual purpose and unfolding. For example, consider this affirmation: "I am a beautiful person."

In the first person, write this affirmation down on one side of a piece of paper. On the other side, write down your mind chatter. Whatever comes up, just write. It could be, "Oh, yeah, have you looked in the mirror today?" Acknowledge the resistance; don't try to resist it. Let it drain from the inside of your being. Keep up this process. Here is an example:

I am a beautiful person
   Oh, yeah, have you looked into a
   mirror today?

I am a beautiful person
   Oh, yeah, have you brushed your
   teeth today?

I am a beautiful person
   Oh, yeah, a little short aren't you?

I am a beautiful person
   Oh, yeah, how about those pounds
   you gained over the holidays?

The dialogue may go on for a whole page. Write it down and get it out. Uncover the barriers to your expression of wholeness and freedom. Eventually monkey mind and your chatterbox is satisfied, cleaned out, cleansed and released. Monkey mind is a Buddhist term — it is the chatter in your mind which distracts you from your hopes, dreams and desires. There will come a time in this process when you feel that you are free, and that the affirmation is the vibration of your soul.

Use the second person to say, "You are a beautiful person." Let monkey mind and chatterbox be released. When that is complete, repeat this using the third person. "She is a beautiful person." Again, release all forms of monkey mind by writing down the resisting thoughts and letting them go.

When you are done, it is extremely important

to use a physical act to eliminate the writings. Use a ritual to demonstrate that you are willing to release whatever stands between you and your desires. Watch a solid piece of paper change form as it goes up in smoke. Use the ashes to feed your plants and realize that good comes from everything. The transmuted form of your fearful thoughts can be the source of beautiful flowers and foliage for your plants. Whatever ritual you choose, make sure no one else will read what you wrote.

Now you can authentically and organically believe the affirmation. It becomes the truth of your soul, your mind and your physical body. In your inner and outer being, you are flowing in union with your highest vibration.

I believe that the call to become a minister and graduating from Unity School of Christianity was a chance to heal my physical and spiritual being. Following this calling allowed me to flow with the purpose of my life. The activities involved with becoming and being a minister served me in the highest and greatest way. These Truth Principals continue to serve me as I teach them to others, while rejoicing in the fact that life is sweet, fun, and filled with the love of God.

I graduated from Unity School of Christianity and was ordained by the Association of Unity Churches on August 13, 1976. On August 14, I started my trip to Memphis, Tennessee for my first assignment as a temporary minister. During my two-week assignment, I did all the things that a minister does in a Southern state with Southern people. I performed my first baptism, first wedding, first official counseling session, first board meeting — my first everything. It was a dynamic time for the Memphis congregation. The members had just decided to sell the old church and build a new one. In those two weeks, I fell in love with the ministry. I also fell in love with the people and customs of the South.

At the end of two weeks, I packed everything into the back seat of my car and took off for my permanent assignment in California. The trip took me across two-thirds of the United States to my destination in Vallejo, California where I looked for a motel room. But there was no room at the inn. I finally just begged a hotel to let me stay in an extra storage room with a bed in it. I cried myself to sleep because things didn't *feel* right. Was this lack of flow simply an appearance that I needed to look past? I made a commitment to Spirit to make this assignment work.

In Vallejo, a study group was taking steps to become a recognized Unity Church. Many legal issues were involved. Our new church had to create a permanent place to meet. Then it needed to obtain a secretary, a mailing permit, and tax exempt status. Taking care of all of this business while getting to know my congregation made this a busy time for me.

For a while, the church office was in my home. I had rented an unfurnished apartment with no clue how I could afford to furnish it. Before the end of three weeks, it was totally filled with beautiful furniture. Some of it was purchased, but most was from an estate in the process of settlement. The furniture was stored in my apartment. It was much nicer than anything I could have purchased.

The Unity congregation was increasing in numbers and making front-page headlines. We rented space from the Sweet Lilly Primitive Baptist Church, a black congregation in a white neighborhood. Their congregation did not believe in music while ours did. They had complete submersion for baptism; we had spiritual baptism. Their minister was a black man. I was a white woman. I worked in the church full time, while he had a full time job and worked in church part time. It appeared as though we had no similarities. We held our service at on Sunday mornings for about an hour while they worshipped the rest of the day.

The Unity congregation had the opportunity to totally redecorate the office and bookstore, located inside the church. The local newspaper called for an interview, complete with photographs. The Baptist minister and I got together before the interview with the newspaper and decided to emphasize our similarities. We spoke of the messages of love, service to humanity, the unity in Unity and of honoring and accepting each other's differences. We celebrated our similarities. What a win/win situation it was! The story of our two congregations received front page coverage. The other minister and I got our pictures in the paper. Isn't God good?!

NOT ALL IS GOOD, BUT
GOOD COMES FROM ALL.

Chapter 17

Lesson in Practice

One of my duties as a minister is to perform wedding ceremonies. Ministry can be challenging, but it can also be a lot of fun. Remember the tattoo story that my brother shared with my family? One time, a couple asked me to perform a wedding at a tattoo parlor. The occasion was filled with fun and laughter, and I still enjoy the memories of that day. The couple joked about paying for the wedding in trade, and asked if I wanted a tattoo. At least, I think they were joking.

When I walked into the tattoo parlor, an African-American man was getting a large orange tiger on his chest. He asked me to pray with him and hold his hand while he was getting the tattoo. I held his hand and waited for the wedding guests to arrive. Afterwards, I turned down the offer of trading for a tattoo because the parlor didn't have the angel I wanted.

The bride and groom slipped out of their sweat suits just before the ceremony, and their appearance was a sight to behold. She had tattoos all over. Her husband-to-be was the artist of the illustrations that covered her body. The bride's white shorts were imprinted with black skulls that showed off her scenic legs. Her T-shirt was black with white skulls on it. The colors of the groom's outfit were the exact inverse. He wore black pants with white skulls and a white T-shirt with black skulls.

The guests attending the wedding were friends of the bride and groom, but no family members were present. The groom decided to call his mother, who lived in Arizona, so she could listen to ceremony. I was holding the phone, the marriage manual, and the rings. The groom's mother was crying. She kept talking, which was distracting, since I was trying to perform the ceremony. There were so many things to juggle that I dropped the phone, and upset the mother who thought something bad had happened. Except for that, everything was fine. After I blessed the rings and the bride and groom kissed, I left quickly. I decided I didn't really want a tattoo.

This tattoo parlor story was included to illustrate the power of words. The universe has many ways of fulfilling ideas. The family joke about my tattoo (which originated years earlier because of my bartending job) almost turned into a reality. Words and thoughts carry across time and eventually manifest. That is why it is so important to be aware of words, and to align your words with the experiences that you want to create.

Shortly after my divorce was finalized, I began doing prayer work to heal the family relationship. My children were confused, and I didn't get to see them regularly because they lived in another state.

From my regression work, I knew that my former husband and I would be tied together in future lifetimes, even as we were in the past. I continued the prayer work after I moved to California.

One Sunday morning, my children, their father, and his wife arrived in California. Their destination was Disneyland, but in the interim they spent three days with me. They attended the Unity service, and I introduced them to my congregation as very special people in my life: my children, their father, and his lovely wife. Heads almost twisted off. Then my congregation realized my extended family was spending the weekend with me. The healing had taken years to accomplish, but I always knew that my spiritual work would manifest in God's time.

I was still driving the car that I manifested some time ago using treasure mapping. Treasure mapping is a technique that channels the creativity of mind and spirit to generate genuine changes on all levels, including the physical. The map is made on construction paper or poster board. Pictures of the circumstances and material things you want to have in your life are glued to the paper. The treasure map acts like a magnet to draw these things into your life. In my case, it was a new car.

My secretary's husband knew a lot about cars, so he went with me to San Francisco to shop for a car. My financing was already arranged with a credit union for a set amount. At the dealership, I saw a car that I couldn't afford. It was a Thunderbird, metallic rose with burgundy leather interior. I was practically drooling looking at the car. My secretary's husband said, "Do you know what is standing between you and that car?" I asked, "What?" He answered, "Desire. How much do you want it?" He grinned and walked away.

The salesman let me take the Thunderbird for a drive. I loved it, and went back in to determine what the cost and payments would be. The dealer sold it to me for the price of a Mustang. I drove away with the car of my dreams at the price that I had negotiated with the credit union. God is good. All the time!

Treasure mapping works. It is actually a form of prayer. Instead of silently or verbally praying, pictures and written words are used as visual cues to help the mind create. Be aware of this when choosing the pictures and words to include on your treasure map.

HOW TO MAKE AN IMAGE BOOK

"Being comes before having."
"First within, then without."

My outer world and all that it contains is merely the visible replica of my inner mind state. If I want to change my life experience, then I must change my thoughts and feelings — I must change my mind.

My self-image defines and creates my life experiences. My experiences on a moment-to-moment basis can be no higher nor lower than that invisible image. My self-image is composed of my thoughts and feelings about myself, and it doesn't matter whether these are conscious or subconscious.

Mind (thinking and feeling) = self-image. Self-image = me, the visible replica of my mind state.

A very powerful and effective method of changing one's self-image is through the use of an Image Book or I AM Book, a book that describes the real me in pictures and words. Another name for this book is a treasure map.

Follow these directions for treasure mapping and you will soon be attracting the situations and circumstances that fulfill your highest dreams:

1. Cut out words and pictures which are descriptive of the real you — your highest self. You may not feel them or believe them now, but they describe how you intend to feel about yourself. The idea is to reach so far beyond your present concepts about yourself and your life that your new ideas almost embarrass you. The pictures that you choose should not include a face, so it will be easier to identify with that new image.

2. Use bold letter words from magazines that can be made into phrases or sentences, such as I pray for – I believe in – I always – I feel – I can – I have – I am – I love – My life is – My dreams are – I will – I want to – I celebrate – I care about – I applaud my – joy – beautiful – exciting – God Truth – Trust – inspiration – spiritual.

3. Create one or more pages on various aspects of your life that you want to change, develop, or expand. Describe inner qualities such as your femininity or masculinity, self-confidence, and spiritual nature. Describe the outer, visible part of you and your life. Include pictures and words that show your desired physical appearance and clothing. Include images that portray you as an effective and loving spouse, parent or friend.

4. If you have a problem area such as lack of order or lack of organization, create a page affirming the order in your life — "I am organized in all things," etc.

5. Read these pages each day and really feel that you are this person with those qualities until dramatic changes take place in your life.

The purpose of this exercise is to call forth qualities which already exist in you, but perhaps have not been seen, felt, or experienced. You are not trying to be like someone else, but are calling forth the highest and best that you already are. This works for manifesting items in your life like the car story earlier in this chapter. Have fun with your treasure map, and believe in miracles.

For years, I have used a prayer technique called "The Master Mind," which is described elsewhere in this book. Before I left for the car dealership to buy my car, my master mind partner called from the Midwest. He said he wanted to support me as he felt I was doing something special that day. When I told him I was buying a car, he said, "If you don't buy a classy car for the classiest lady I know, you are selling yourself short."

That support from my prayer partner combined with the universe to say "yes," and those forces produced the car of my dreams. The dealership gave me a higher priced car for the price that my credit union had agreed to finance. God is good all the time.

Though I served the California church for two years, it never felt like home. From the time I arrived in California until I decided to leave, I fell and stumbled frequently. When walking on the sidewalk or even just across a floor, I would fall. My downstairs neighbors thought I drank, because they frequently heard me falling. The very minute that I decided to leave California, I stopped falling. I didn't know where I was going, but Spirit guided me to send out my resume, and I sensed that everything would work out.

A week later, a call came from the Memphis Unity Church. Their minister was resigning and they invited me to come out for a visit. Although other candidates applied, I got it. Right after my ordination, I had served in Memphis temporarily, and now I would return to serve in the church that felt like my spiritual home. I applied the Universal Principles while ministering in California. I will always be grateful for my ministry in California and the lessons that I learned. I looked forward to practicing these lessons in Memphis.

NOT ALL IS GOOD, BUT
GOOD COMES FROM ALL.

Chapter 18

Revelation through Regression

There were many tools which assisted me in healing my life. One particular area, the circumstances surrounding my conception and birth, remained as a troubling part of my life. When I was in my thirties, I experienced a past life regression. When I was the minister in Vallejo, California and looking for a guest speaker, I thought about asking Dr. Ruth Wambach to speak at the church. She was a regressionist who helped people to experience their past lives. I called her to find out exactly what she did. She said, "I can't begin to explain it all — why don't you come and experience it?" She told me to bring a blanket, because the participants would lie on the floor.

The day of the seminar, Dr. Wambach informed everyone that she was writing a book, and wanted to include the results of this session in her book. No names would be used, so everyone agreed and signed release forms. Then, seventeen of us spread our blankets on the hard tile floor. The lights were turned out, except for a small lamp near Dr. Wambach. She sat at one end of the room and read a script, guiding us through our past life experience. She led us into a timeframe at an unnamed area of the earth. She instructed us to look around and get an idea of where we lived in that time. Then we were told to look at our hands to see if we were male or female, large or small. We looked at our skin color and at our feet to see what kind of footwear we wore.

As the experience progressed, we were instructed to touch our hair, and to look into a reflecting pool of water to see ourselves. The session guided us through various time periods. Dr. Wambach's research for her book dealt with tracing the flow of the population from one part of the world to another. Personal stories were of no interest to her. She only wanted to know what we looked like, our nationality, where we lived and what the geography of the area was like.

In the last episode of the regression, we were told to ask our higher selves if it was appropriate to reveal the purpose of our present lives. Up until this time, I thought I was experiencing a very vivid movie provided by an active imagination. The inner journey would begin at the time of conception and bring us through the birth process. When Dr. Wambach asked us to go back to our conception, I found myself watching a very unpleasant scenario. I saw my conception.

I understood that the person who would be my biological father was no more than a sperm donor. He caused my life to begin by forcing himself on my mother. He raped her and hurt her. There was a stench of alcohol hanging like a fog, and he was extremely drunk. Being present at my conception and witnessing it allowed me to have

134

greater compassion for my mother. I received insight into my deep connection to her. We had been sisters in another life and then mother and daughter. I experienced a soul connection with my soon-to-be physical mother in this life. This violence associated with my conception has affected my whole life, especially my relationships with others. My mother cried a lot and did not want me. I often withdrew my energy from the process of building my body. She didn't want me, and I wasn't sure I wanted to be born.

During this regression, I saw the natal decisions that my soul faced. On a soul level, we have what might be called a spiritual board of advisers. They guide us during our transitions from one life to the next life, which holds the next set of lessons. I didn't want this terrible conception or this constant feeling of rejection from my mother as part of my lessons. I had a meeting with my spiritual advisers. They gently, lovingly reminded that we always have free will about our physical embodiment and our physical birth.

My spiritual advisors suggested that fulfilling the contract I had with my mother would be very good for both of us. This lifetime would be filled with great soul accomplishments for everyone presently in my life and in the future. I remember so well how I felt after this meeting. I decided, "I will fulfill this duty, but I won't enjoy the experience." It was like a floor that has to be scrubbed. You are not going to have a good time — you are just glad when it's done. Another assumption was that *life would be hard, but I could and would endure the experience.*

135

Finally, I observed my birth. I did not enter my physical body until my mother was in labor. When I emerged, the cord was wrapped around my neck and my physical body went into distress. I withdrew my essence and witnessed the rest of my birth from the top of a green instrument cabinet in the delivery room. When my bottom was smacked (rather hard, because my blue color had the doctors fearing that I couldn't breathe on my own) I re-entered the body that would be my home for this lifetime.

Does that give you a deeper understanding about abortions? There is no right or wrong in a woman's decision. The choices are whether to keep the child, give it up for adoption or abort it. Regression and my counseling experience lead me to believe the decisions must be made on an individual basis. I believe every decision is the "right" one for the mother and fetus. Some souls enter the womb immediately upon conception, just like some people live in a house while it is being built around them. Some live in the house after it has been completed. Some just check on the progress as the child is put together cell by cell from the building materials selected by the energy to accomplish the task. There is a contract or commitment, which you bring with you to accomplish in this lifetime.

After the regression session, I called my mother to ask her if she almost lost me during her pregnancy. She told me about spotting and bleeding. There was a fear of miscarriage, and my mother was told she needed complete bed rest. She was told not to sew the flannel diapers and other baby things, which were handmade in those days. Suddenly she asked, "How did you know this? I never told anyone. No one else knew."

Mom was amazed when I told her about my session with the regression, the doctor and the discoveries I had during the process. She affirmed everything that I saw and felt about my birth, including that the cord was wrapped around my neck, and that I turned blue.

I was born at 2:45 a.m. February 4, in Fargo, North Dakota. I remember the light being so bright when I was born I felt like it hurt my eyes. This was the most real thing about the regression. Dr. Ruth Wambach said, "You are now born." I opened my eyes and thought that someone had flooded the room with a bright light. The room was not lit up at all. This made the whole session seem so believable for me. Thank God I changed my mind and chose to live in this physical body. I continue to fulfill life commitments and contracts that I made before my physical birth into this lifetime.

The strength of the power of thought carries through until you re-decide and make another decision. Many times we make decisions that last throughout our whole lives. The powerful message I received from this regression was to bring this message to others. The plan continues to unfold as to how I can achieve this in my life as a minister. I take one breath and one step at a time.

NOT ALL IS GOOD, BUT
GOOD COMES FROM ALL.

Chapter 19

The Why of My Life

I believe my purpose in this life is to learn to love while being of service to humankind. In time, I learned to love the spirit of the man who raped my mother. I didn't like what he did, but I gave thanks and loved the spirit within him. I conceived my children, gave birth to them, raised them to a certain age and loved them enough to release them so we could all complete our agreed-upon assignments in this life.

Though a pattern of drama surrounded many events in my life, I passed those tests with and because of love. I was able to forgive the wounds of the past — and the people who wounded me — by working with prayer for many months. A breakthrough happened when my ex-husband, his wife and my children stayed overnight in my home and attended church with me the next morning. The reconciliation was a healing for all of us.

My children's father and his wife did a great job raising our children. When the children were young, I wasn't a great demonstrator of wealth. My children had the advantages of a stable and financially strong home with their father. He instilled in them a respect for education. The adjustment for children during a divorce is extremely difficult and they act out their pain at that time. My children were no different. It took an understanding of what they were going through to be able to make their adjustments easier.

My daughter is the type of person who has never met a stranger and makes friends easily. She has visited many of the Unity churches where I have been a minister: California, Tennessee, Indiana, Kansas. My son did not visit very often. One year, when my ministry was in Memphis, Tennessee, David did come to visit. The main reason for his visit was to find out why his father and I had divorced. I tried to explain, but I don't think he understood at that time.

Some years later, when David was in Air Force boot camp, he came to Memphis for a holiday. We met at a friend's house and stayed there together. During this time, David spoke with his father by telephone. His father was having marital problems, and asked for David to help. My ex-husband's wife had left him, and he wanted David to convince her to return home. He also wanted David to talk to her about her excessive drinking, and convince her to be a responsible wife. My son was very depressed after the conversation.

David and I went out to dinner that night to talk and spend time together privately. I reminded him of some specific happy times we had together when we were a family, but he didn't remember those times. David didn't think his childhood was particularly happy. I spent some time enumerating all his father's good qualities. I wanted David to know how I felt — that his father had done a great job of raising him and his sister. That only seemed to confuse David. If his dad was that wonderful, why didn't I stay married to him? Finally, I found the right words. I told David that a good father does not necessarily make a good husband. When I looked in David's eyes, I noticed a change, and it seemed as if he understood. I hoped David would realize it wasn't his responsibility to fix his father's relationship problems — it wasn't in the past, and it wasn't now.

My life has been a series of learning experience, and some of those experiences are more fun than others. Whatever "normal" may mean to other people, my life feels normal to me. It took many life lessons to realize my life's purpose: to learn to love without conditions. No matter what someone is doing or how that person is acting, I must react from a place of compassion and love. By taking the higher view and seeing the big picture, I can move on to the next life lesson, and do my life's work. I can do that because I know in my heart that everything happens for a purpose and good comes from all.

NOT ALL IS GOOD, BUT
GOOD COMES FROM ALL.

Chapter 20

My Ministry

I refer to my Tennessee ministry as the Pink Ministry, although I never quite determined how this reference was created for my Memphis church. Perhaps it was because of the visualization script I recited as a guided meditation during the service. It often included a bubble of pink light, which works well for many kinds of healing. At that time, I also wore pink clothes and accessories on Sunday. One day, a woman in the congregation asked, "Do you always wear nail polish to match your car?" Unknown to me, the rumor going around the church was that everything in my house was pink, including my sheets and telephones. People sometimes made excuses just so they could use my bedroom phone — they were disappointed to discover that it wasn't pink. Although I loved my metallic rose car, I certainly was not obsessed with this color.

I loved my Memphis ministry. The congregation changed in two years from a small number of people to an overflow crowd on Sunday mornings. The Wednesday night services went from a handful of people to an average of seventy-five or more. The church's income quadrupled during my time as minister, and all outstanding loans were paid. The church facility, reflecting the vitality of the congregation, acquired new roofing, new paint, and a new parking lot.

Some unusual events occurred during my ministry in Tennessee. These events provided me the chance to practice my faith as a student as well as a teacher.

When I took over as minister at the Memphis church, the bank statements had not been reconciled for over two years. There was no way to know where the church stood financially. The Board agreed a volunteer was needed to clean up the records. A new person in the congregation was in business as an accountant. Of course, I didn't know her lifestyle or background, but she invited me out to dinner and volunteered to do the books. In my eagerness to have the financial records updated, I accepted her offer, even though my judgment and intuition warned me of problems to come.

During that meeting, I failed to set boundaries and didn't process the accountant's words — while describing how she could help the church, this lady mentioned that she had "done people in." At the time, it wasn't clear to me that I would be her next target. After a few months working on the books, she became a pivotal decision maker as an active member and church treasurer. She wielded a great deal of power.

During a counseling appointment with me, she revealed that she was in love with me and wanted a relationship. I acknowledged her feelings, but told her firmly, "Thanks, but no thanks."

She left, but later called for another appointment. In my mind, the issue of having a relationship was over, but this woman wouldn't take no for an answer. When she came to my office, she used the same kind of lines that an infatuated man might have used, telling me she would take care of everything and would show me the best times of my life. I repeated my previous words: "Thanks, but no thanks."

When she approached me the third time about a relationship, she told me, "I will have you, or I will have your job. You will not remain a minister."

For the final time, I said, "Thanks, but no thanks." She left the office and I thought that was the end of it. Because of my naiveté and inability to maintain boundaries, I was taken by surprise when she followed through on her threats. She told key people in the congregation that I was embezzling money from the church. It wasn't just me she attacked — she spread the rumor that I was a lesbian, and claimed I was involved with other women in the ministry. As if that wasn't enough, she said I was also having affairs with married men. I would have been a very busy person to engage in all of these diverse activities.

In one of her schemes to "save" the church from me, she accused me of stealing money from the church's checking account. Even though I was a qualified check signer, I had only signed one check the whole time I was in Memphis. Further, it would have been very difficult to steal the Sunday donations. The money was counted by two ushers and again by the secretary. The treasurer wrote out any checks that had two signatures on them.

With this obsessed woman as their leader, a small group of people tried to have me removed as minister of the church. Three of them came into the church to confiscate all the records, including the church stamps. Everything! They chose a day that the Association of Unity Churches would be closed. There was no way for me to contact the association.

In order to take responsibility for this situation, I had to examine what was creating the conflict with this group of people. It was the expansion of the congregation. Although most people wanted the church to grow, a few didn't. I became the focal point for them of the things they didn't like.

I called a board meeting to offer my resignation. If I was the problem, I was going to remove myself. The following Sunday, I resigned. I based my whole sermon around endings. People cried. As a surprise, they planned a big celebration for my second anniversary with the church. It was painful. Before dinner, over one hundred sixty signatures had been collected rejecting my resignation. At a special board meeting I agreed to stay on as minister, but I wouldn't go back to the pulpit until the conflict was resolved. While I remained absent from the pulpit, I hired a number of different people to lead the services.

A liaison committee from the Association of Unity Churches met with the group of people who wanted me leave in order to hear their concerns. After much time, money, effort, and energy, thirteen people left the church. This woman was one of them. Praise God!

The breakaway group started their own study group. Because of the whole situation, one Unity teacher had her license revoked. It would never be reinstated again because of the role she played in splintering the church. That didn't end my harassment. The police warned me how hateful this group had become. Sometimes I left my own home for my own safety. The woman (whose romantic advances I had refused) would call my home and blow a whistle into the phone every two hours day and night. She used a different pay phone each time so she couldn't be traced. With the obsession of having me or having my job, she sometimes parked outside my house to spy on me. She kept track of my activities and my visitors, then made up stories about what was going on.

I accepted total responsibility for this series of events. It happened because of my lack of judgment, my inexperience just coming out of Ministerial School, and because I didn't realize you can predict someone's future actions based on their past actions. If I had listened to this woman's own words about the numerous suits she had engaged in, I would have seen the red flags. I assumed too much. Perception of power is in the person who perceives, whether it is genuine or not. This experience taught me to be very cautious about setting and keeping boundaries.

One of the great things that came out of this experience was the strength of the church. Its members grew, and its financial strength grew. The thirteen people who left thought they could bankrupt the church. Instead, after their departure, the church flourished. The entire building was refurbished. Sometimes you have to cut out the major problem before you can work on your healing. When the thirteen people left, they took their negativity with them, which allowed the church to bloom and unfold in marvelous ways.

The conflicts at the Memphis Unity Church provided opportunities for me to let go of the past, and I found the willingness to do so. It was such a lesson for me to see how people make choices in their lives. I saw the unity in Unity, embodied in the Memphis area congregation. As for those who caused the negative energy in and around me during that time, I released them into God's light and love and claimed the blessing from that situation. I know that right where they are, God is and all is well.

NOT ALL IS GOOD, BUT
GOOD COMES FROM ALL.

Chapter 21

Word Power

For years, I resisted the call to become a minister. When I finally committed to my ministry, my physical and spiritual healing began, which allowed me to flow with the true purpose of my life. Lessons are only words unless you absorb and apply them, in which case they become life-changing. My life lessons served me in the highest way. If I had only one chance to address the world, everyone would hear me in his or her native tongue. My message would be to make people aware of the power that words have, whether as silent thoughts or a verbal commitments. If you want to change, improve, or transform your life, start with changing, improving and transforming your words.

Your life in the present moment is the result of words and thoughts you have repeated over and over again. The power of those words attracted the experiences you are having now. Whatever you utter becomes your outer experience. God created the world with the power of the spoken word. God did this to prove that people create their own worlds in the same way. God gave us the ability to name everything. As we go about naming everything in our lives as good or bad, that makes it so. We do it with the power of the spoken word. The facts to support whatever we speak then manifest. We can say, "See, I am right. These facts prove that I am right." Had we considered a different word to speak, we could have gathered the facts to "prove" that word as valid.

When I spoke in jest and protest about not wanting to grow old, I started saying that I wasn't going to live to see forty. As a child, I considered forty to be old. After all, who would want to live to be that old? When I was in my middle thirties, I created a condition in my physical body that could have claimed my life had I not taken a different stand on the matter. My new words were these: "Kings X, God. I have changed my mind. Forty is young." My inner work wasn't done just by speaking. I also had to change many of my self-images that were engraved in my mind.

Using the power of visualization, I began creating new mental images. I started "seeing" my body as being in a state of perfect health. I would look at a children's book of anatomy to see how a healthy body was supposed to look. Then I superimposed that picture on my body. I did this until I felt and looked as good as the picture, until there was no separation of one from the other. I didn't do this just once or twice a week or a month; I did the visualizations every day, faithfully for nine months. I visualized the doctor and my friends telling me I was healed and healthy.

Using the power of the spoken word is a way to ask for what you want in your life. Sometimes during this work, monkey mind can get in with chatter at each level of development to undermine your efforts. Use the releasing technique described earlier to work through monkey mind and dissolve its effects.

At some point, monkey mind becomes quiet. Nothing else comes to the surface. At that point, you *know* that your affirmations can take root and become living breathing words as your life experience. You will know them as true facts in *your* life, not as unmanifested *truths*. The pure potentiality of your being will have manifested into physical reality. Finish the affirmation exercise with a ritual to release the fearful thoughts that were written.

With the power of your spoken words, you are now free to use your affirmations supported by the passion and power of the Universe. Get ready to witness the miracles that will take place in your life experience. Play this simple game of Erase-and-Replace with a friend.

Many times when we speak we don't hear our own words. There are so many phrases that do not generate powerful life experiences. Out of habit, we keep repeating them and wonder why our lives are not going in the direction we want.

Have you used any of these phrases?

I was tickled to death.
I came home and crashed.
I got on the airplane and crashed.
She was drop-dead gorgeous

151

She looks smashing in that outfit.
He makes my blood boil.
I could just blow my top when that happens.
He/she made me so angry.
That makes me sick to my stomach to see that happen.
You are going to be the death of me.
What rock did you crawl out from under?
I was hit by a two-by-four.
That cracks me up.
I have a deadline to meet.

You may realize you have heard or use many more statements like these. When you enlist the help of a friend, she/he can help draw your attention to your unconscious use of these words. You gently say, "erase and replace" and choose new words that describe what you want to manifest. Too often, people operate on automatic pilot. Become aware of how you seal your own fate with your own spoken words. Even if you deny that you mean it, your mind believes it as truth because you said it. Your mind operates as if it were true. Repetition gives power to words you may not want in your life. Power, passion and repetition in the first, second and third person are how we create our world — both the world we want and the world we don't want.

NOT ALL IS GOOD, BUT
GOOD COMES FROM ALL.

Chapter 22

Purpose

Everything, everyone, every event, every situation has purpose in your life. The events you don't want to happen, the person you don't like, all enter into your life for a reason. They are in your life for you to experience because of your vibrational invitation. You may not even remember inviting, calling or telling a person to do something or act in some way. That doesn't matter — you still will find yourself in the middle of the drama. The person or situation is in your life by divine appointment, created with advice and guidance from your higher power.

We all do this. Some of us do it more consciously than others. If we pay attention to our emotions, we can start to understand how those unconscious invitations are issued. It's easy to forget or hide emotions in our minds, especially when we don't want to take full responsibility for our lives. Lack of action is also action. An example of this is not accepting a role which is placed on our path. We have called it, we need it, but then we reject it. Sometimes it takes courage to face the invitations that we send to the universe. At those times, it is vital that we focus on our higher good.

A change of awareness can help us to interact with those difficult people and events that we chose to manifest in our lives.

It took me many years of studying spiritual principles to understand the concept of "stay and play," or perhaps better called "stay and pray." I was strong-willed as a youngster, and later learned to stand firm when I believed in something, regardless of what society or an individual said about what I should or should not believe. One of those decisions meant leaving a marriage so I could pursue my life commitment. I see now that I created the marriage drama. The roles played by other people were played because they agreed to play them with me. Getting attached to the role is what brought me the pain and suffering. Pain is a part of being human. Pain can't be avoided in this life on planet earth. It's the suffering that is optional. I now recognize that I don't have to suffer in this life. Life is to be enjoyed, not just to be endured. That is my purpose and mission in life. I am so grateful that I took advice from my advisors and agreed to stay.

If you are searching for your life's purpose, it is a great time to journal. You can journal in many ways. Write in a notebook or record a tape, or write in a word processing program on a computer. This is a story of your path, of your walk, of remembering who you are. Sometimes that story starts with questions. *Who am I? What am I doing here?* And this begins the wonderful search. Journaling is a spiritual tool that raises the quality of your life.

It is fun to be here in a physical form during such an exciting time on this earth, doing things that make a difference in the lives of others. I love and enjoy life. That doesn't mean some days aren't difficult, but generally life is to be celebrated. Most of the time, it gets better and better. God *is* good all the time, but there is nothing wrong with questioning this. Questioning provides time for our souls to search deeply — to the edges of the universe — for their connection with the wonder of God.

Life cannot be taken. Its form can change, but life energy remains even when someone's body is no longer alive.

I realized that even outside of the physical body we have *free will*. Know that with *free will* comes choice.

NOT ALL IS GOOD, BUT
GOOD COMES FROM ALL.

Chapter 23

The Goodness of God

I believe in the absolute goodness of the universal force called God, Love, Light, Primal energy, Prana, the Higher power, universal energy, or whatever name you prefer. God is not only good to me and for me; *God is purely good* — period. Even when things happen that do not appear to be "good," my heart and soul knows that *good* is the only quality that exists. If I resist what is happening, I create more suffering and pain for myself. Even that is not bad unless my strong opinion invests energy to "prove" my opinion of bad. It is important to invest energy looking for solutions involving the good that I can experience in my life.

We put ourselves into an inner prison and attract restrictive situations if we resist what is. Resistance deflects the good that wants to enter our lives. You can do something constructive to experience freedom even if a locked door says you are a prisoner. Let me share an example of a man who was a prisoner of war for seven years in North Vietnam. Major James Nesmeth was imprisoned in a cage approximately four and one half feet high and five feet long. He couldn't stand up or lie down in these confining conditions. This was a very factual and true prison for Major Nesmeth. During his imprisonment, he could see no one, talked to no one, and experience virtually no physical activity. The first few months in the cage, he resisted being there, a normal reaction which most would follow in the same situation. He did nothing but hope and pray for his release. Prayer is a limitless tool when used properly, but the subtle difference between proper and improper use must be understood. Praying and hoping from a point of desperation does not improve a situation mentally or emotionally. If that was his only method of coping, Major Nesmeth would lose his sanity and probably his life.

So what did he do? Major Nesmeth learned not to resist a reality that he couldn't escape. He recognized that true freedom lies within, and learned to use his power of imagination. One of the things he did was to visualize himself playing golf. Every single day, he selected the country club of his dreams and played eighteen holes of golf. Take a few minutes and imagine playing golf. Major Nesmeth played golf seven days a week for four hours a day. For seven years, he played eighteen holes of golf daily. If my calculations are correct, that is 10,164 total hours of golf during the time that he was a prisoner of war.

Before his capture, Major Nesmeth dreamed of knowing how to play golf well. He relived his dream every day for seven years. The dream that kept him alive took twenty strokes off his game. After his release, he shot a 74 on his first time out on a golf course, even though his body had deteriorated from inactivity. Amazing as this story is, you too have this same power within you to use good thoughts during bad times. Major Nesmeth learned that resisting reality could have driven him insane. Through the power of visualization and imagination, he not only saved his sanity and his physical life but he improved his golf game. Does this sound too simple? Not if you understand the power of refusing to be a victim — even in extreme circumstances.

Sometimes people are in a prison of their own personal choices in life. They resist being there. They find excuses to explain why the things that are happening aren't their fault. They believe "the system" is out to get them. This attitude causes them to retain what they resist or don't want. In other words, they keep doing something to attract the same people or situations. This can continue over and over for years. The prison is created by their own thoughts. Without resistance, the power of the mind — the power of imagination — can free people from whatever prison (real or created) confines them.

The laws of the universe *always* work. Never is there a time on earth when gravity (or the law of cause and effect) stops working. Some people say prayer and affirmations don't work for them. Life just happens to them. Why should they put in the effort to discipline themselves and their thinking if it really doesn't make a difference anyway? If you cling to this way of thinking, you are avoiding responsibility for your life. By failing to take responsibility, you ultimately give your power away. You can become a victim and say, "My life doesn't work." You can really give your power away by saying things like, "The devil made me do it," or "I just lost control and it happened." How about this one: "I did it because it is God's will." All of these statements make you helpless. It is up to you to do things differently in your life.

Changing your energy changes you and the way you react to life. The circumstances that bring a person to the point of incarceration result from the law of cause and effect. Let's look at how this may work in your life. Unity has a saying, "Thoughts held in mind produce after their kind." People say, "I have never thought of xyz disease, and yet the doctor told me I have xyz disease. How could I have held those thoughts in mind if I had never even heard of that disease?" The key words to consider are "after their kind." This means a lack of ease produces a lower, slower and denser vibration rather than the higher, faster and clearer vibration that indicates health. A disease or lack of ease is experienced in your body. You don't have to think precisely of that exact disease to have a slower and denser energy vibration show up as a lack of ease in your body.

Here's a story illustrating this principle. A woman had a panic attack while driving across a long bridge. She drove on this bridge regularly, and never before had a problem. Why did she have a panic attack so powerful that she wondered if she could make it to the other side of the bridge? She even wanted to stop her car and hide under the dashboard because of the fear she felt. On closer examination, she realized she was attracting fearful vibrations because she was emanating those same vibrations. Her neighbor's house had been broken into. Because of fear, the woman started looking at prices and features of security equipment. She thought about buying window bars for her home. She didn't make a purchase, but her vibration was full of fear. In this state, she was receptive to fearful vibrations emanating from other people who had ever crossed that bridge. The vibration of fear has a lower, slower, denser energy than the vibration of positive emotions. Once the woman recognized this, she was able to laugh at her self-creation. She was no longer a victim of security systems or panic attacks on bridges. She recognized her freedom to select a different vibration — that of love. Love has a higher, faster, purer and cleaner vibration of positive energy.

In order to assist your own healing, you can contribute by changing your energy vibration. This can work in conjunction with following the instructions of your medical professionals. Think and feel about what you do want, not what you don't want. Think healthy, happy, fun thoughts about something in your life to change your discomfort to a higher, faster vibration. If you focus on what you don't want, you get more of what you don't want. The reverse is also true.

Research shows that the healthy body and the diseased body have different frequencies. The vibration for a healthy body is 62-78 hertz(Hz).

Bone frequency is 38-43(Hz)
Spiritual frequencies range from 92-360(Hz).

161

A lower and slower vibration creates
the attraction of dis-ease (disease)
such as:
Cold symptoms 58 Hz
Flu symptoms 57 Hz
Candida 55 Hz
Epstein Bar 52 Hz
Cancer 42 Hz
Processed/canned food 0 Hz
Fresh produce up to 15 Hz
Dry Herbs 12-22 Hz

Essential oils are also helpful in raising the body's vibration. I have heard that burning sage heightens sensuality and helps to connect partners on more than just a physical level.

Another good supplement for raising vibration is this super food:

Super Blue Green Algae 52-320 Hz

Information for this was obtained from Dr. Young's book entitled, *Aromatherapy: An Essential Beginning.*

Being in a state of sadness or depression, like negative thoughts, produces a slower, denser vibration. It slows the Hertz down within our energy body. Whatever we vibrate, we attract; we then magnetically attract disease or sickness — even though that isn't what we want in our lives. Thoughts influence our frequency. Negative thoughts lower our frequency by 12 Hz. Positive thoughts raise it. Prayer and meditation increase our frequency by 15 or more Hz. Thoughts and feelings cause action. Action causes results.

We are three-fold beings consisting of body, mind and spirit. It takes caring attention to all three levels in order to maintain a healthy life. Becoming a blended being brings harmony and balance to our experience. If any one of the three is out of balance, that throws the whole system off. That means that paying attention to what you put into your body temple is as important as paying attention to what you think. Some people believe as long as we take care of the spiritual and the mental levels, the body will remain healthy. For a time, this appears to be true. Our body is a miracle machine, a great wonder to behold with all it does for us, so we often take it for granted. We usually take better care of our automobile than we do of our body temple. We change our car's oil on a regular basis; we put in high-octane fuel, and have regular check-ups. With our body, we consume junk food, which takes care of the hunger for the moment. We pretend that all is well. Eating junk food is like putting dirty fuel into your car and expecting it to run well. It just doesn't work that way in real life.

Blessing food changes its vibrational structure. The food becomes a complete blessing for your body, emotions and spirit.s. What you eat comes from the light and goes to the light. A good example is milk. Grass receives sunshine. Cows eat grass. Cows give milk, we drink milk therefore we are drinking in the light. A carrot is light energy manifested as a carrot. Hamburger is light energy manifested as meat. Hold your hands over your food to bless it as pure light to enhance your physical, mental and emotional Light Body. Always name and claim your ideal healthy body weight at the time of blessing your food. For example: "I, Thelma, respectfully bless this food of Light for my vibrational healthy energetic youthful body of (ideal weight) pounds. I attain and maintain this Light Body with amazing ease and fun in eating."

Most people have the belief that they have to be sick to die and leave their body. This is false. We can graduate without having to go through sickness. It is very important that we don't try to figure out other people's thoughts that caused some dis-ease (disease) within their body. Provide the people with information when and if appropriate, allow them to do the research and discover for themselves. People often cannot see in what ways they are responsible for creating the life situations that they experience.

One of the greatest things you can do for another person is to acknowledge and accept their perspective — even though you may have another view of a situation. Unless they want more information, your efforts to change their way of thinking only create tension. The person may feel a need to defend their beliefs and will come up with all kinds of justification for those beliefs. This just serves to solidify their personal opinions and beliefs even more. It isn't easy to be still when you see a friend or a loved one heading for a cliff. You want to suggest a new direction or new way of thinking. It is better for them, and for you, to do your work in the space of silence rather than trying to change them.

People will continue in the same direction they are headed. Gently share with them what you see about the effects of staying on that course. If they ignore your words, and their actions show that they are continuing on the same path, you must step aside. You must allow them to do what they are doing and to go where they are going. In terms of your own spirituality, this is an opportunity to stop judging people and how they manage their own situations. Later, there may be an opportunity to help, but right now, your interference will just cause resentment.

You can help people by holding them in "The Light." This means holding them in a higher, faster, purer vibration of good — and that doesn't mean your opinion of what their good may be. You do this without speaking a word. This is how our friend Jesus Christ created the miracles seen in the New Testament. When people came to Jesus to ask for help, Jesus did not become part of the problem. He didn't ask questions, sympathize with the person, or tell them how terrible the problem was. Jesus did not look at the problem. He looked beyond appearances and *saw* the person, whole and free. Jesus saw them free to name and claim their own wholeness, their own higher, faster, purer vibration of health, wellness, and the good they desired.

Jesus instructed us to not judge by appearances. Appearances can hypnotize us. We may think there is no way out of a problem. We think we are stuck with it until someone else does something to get us out of the problem. Jesus, the Christ, had the ability to see the wholeness of the person. Jesus looked beyond the appearance of the current situation, even to the point of being able to look beyond death. When Lazarus was in the tomb, Jesus looked beyond the initiation called death to the resurrection of the physical body. In all circumstances, Jesus Christ saw beyond the problems of the people who came to him or were brought to him for healing.

When I take the time to look at the meaning of the words, I can appreciate the teachings of the New Testament. Jesus, the man, was born of Mary. This man of Nazareth was the Savior of humankind according to present day Christian belief. Metaphysically, Jesus is the I AM in humankind. Jesus is the self, the directive power, raised to divine understanding to power the I AM identity. Jesus came to connect the thinker with the True Source of thought. Jesus of Nazareth was a spiritual reformer with a mission from on High. Jesus had an insight into the mysteries of people immersed in the sense of living. Jesus is the Way-shower who came to awaken humanity to the possibilities of its own nature. Jesus came to bear witness to the Truth.

Christ is the perfect idea of God in humankind. Christ is the incarnating principle of humankind. Jesus is the name that represents an individual expression of the Christ idea. Christ existed long before Jesus was born. It was the Christ Mind in Jesus that exclaimed, "and now, Father, glorify thou me with thine own self with the glory which I had with thee before the world was." (John 17:5)

Christ abides in each person as potential perfection. Christ in you, the true light, which guides every person coming into the world as it is and ever has been in all humankind. This is "Christ in you, the hope of glory." (Col. 1:27)

Christ is the perfect idea of God for humankind. Jesus is the perfect expression of the divine idea of humankind. Jesus Christ is a union of the two, the idea and the expression. In other words, Jesus is the perfect person demonstrated.

Jesus' prayers were answered because Jesus always dwelt in the consciousness of perfect harmony with God. When we ask in Jesus' name, it is with an earnest desire for that consciousness which Jesus possessed. In the name and nature of Jesus we pray. The Christ within each of us is ever seeking perfect expression. It is our commitment to have our minds clear and be receptive with a willing eye, ear and heart. We are willing and committed to allow this energy to flow through us. This harmonious relationship between God and humankind is attained by prayer, meditation, and entering the Silence. Charles Fillmore states in *Revealing Word* that we attain harmony by constantly affirming God's Presence and Power. This creates a higher, finer, faster vibration of good.

In short, Jesus is the man; Christ is the ideal within everyone. Jesus knew the ideal of God so perfectly that He knew He was Jesus Christ, the perfect blending. You too, have the Christ in you; so you become (your name) Christ. The life Jesus lived and the energy that flowed through Him lets us know He is our friend. He cared enough to show us the way to follow Him. Jesus doesn't want to be worshipped in the sense that He was the only one who did what He did. Jesus wants to be honored and embraced for teaching and doing what He said everyone could do. Jesus is our elder brother, even our savior as He shows us how to save ourselves from sin.

My favorite definitions of sin are Self Inflicted Nonsense (s.i.n.) or useless, unnecessary suffering, or missing the mark of perfection. John the Baptist told us, *"Repent,"* meaning change your mind and go in another direction. Go in another direction with your thinking and feelings. In so doing, you can follow Jesus Christ to accomplish your mission and your purpose in life.

Love is a good protection for you. Trusting God to be your security system gives you peace of mind and calmness of spirit. Surround your home in a bubble of the white light of the living, loving Christ. This is a higher, faster, purer vibration through which the lower, slower vibration of fear cannot enter. You are safe, secure and protected. This has become my daily intention and my regular affirmation. "I, Thelma am safe, secure and protected." I say this when I am home, in an automobile, a hotel, wherever I am. I want the higher, faster, and finer vibration to be where I am. I want this vibration to go with me, or where I plan to go. I know that I could walk through something dangerous and not be harmed. This is where the Power of Positive Thinking is such a wonderful foundation. In this way you are building self-esteem, love and compassion.

I have the tools required to accomplish a goal set before me. I allow love to flow from my heart center while relaxing from my point of power, the Divine order center point. This point of power is about two inches below the navel. The Ancients tell us that is where the mind, body, and spirit come together in the physical body. Charles Fillmore, co-founder of the Unity Movement, placed the Power of Divine Order in that place within the body. The Japanese call it the Ki from Aikido. The Chinese call it Chi or the Hari point. You can use this as your point of power by relaxing into that space. You become anchored so no one can use your energy against you. No one can throw you off balance mentally, emotionally, physically or even spiritually. If I stay in my head, fear comes and seems to overpower me. So I am gentle with myself and receive the energy through the power frame of the heart and anchoring it in the Divine Order point.

From the Divine Order point I can speak the word for a safe, secure and protected experience for myself. I like to think of it as a pyramid. The tip point of the pyramid is at the throat level where Charles Fillmore places the power point explaining the power of the spoken word. The base of the pyramid is at the heart center. The wisdom center is the solar plexus area. The tip or reversal of the pyramid is the divine order point or *Ki*. When all these energy points are aligned, you can do anything, be anywhere and still be safe, secure and protected. You can accomplish whatever your goal may be as you raise your energy from that lower, slower, denser energy. Your Light will be shining, and you will be a blessing for all that your energy touches. You become a conductor of Light.

You can do an experiment with this energy point just below the navel. This spot is the little soft spot a few fingertips below your navel. You will want a friend to help you with this experiment. Stand behind the person and put your arms just below the chest, and pick them up. Have them stand with their back to you and feet about eighteen inches apart. Ask the volunteer to think about something they don't like or something they fear. Or they can just think about what they read in the newspaper or what they had for breakfast. As the volunteer keeps thinking you attempt to lift them up. Watch their amazement when you can very easily lift them up. Easily, effortlessly you can lift their physical body.

Now ask them to relax and give gentle attention to that power point about two inches below the navel. Repeat the exercise again. Now you can be amazed at how much heavier they have become. Usually you can't even budge them at all. If you are able to move them, it certainly isn't as easy as the first time. Try this with a number of people and have people try it with you. You will get the feel of being in that point of power where no one can throw you off balance. A small person can pick up a two hundred pound person when that person is in his head. However, you can't budge a small child whose attention is focused at the Divine Order point in their body. It feels good to anchor your power and not become the victim of life.

NOT ALL IS GOOD, BUT
GOOD COMES FROM ALL.

Chapter 24

Communications

How do people communicate with each other? Discovering that only seven percent of communication involves spoken words was a shock to me.

Facial Expression	35%
Body (physiology)	23%
Total Body	*58%*
plus	
Tone of voice	35%
Words	7%
Total	*100%*

If you are like me, you want to believe the words, but this can create unnecessary suffering because it doesn't take the whole picture into consideration. A person who has been beaten by a spouse gets in great trouble by believing the words of the perpetrator. The words are said, "I'm sorry. I will never do that again." Within a short time, the same actions are repeated. The spouse said the abuse would never happen again, and yet it did. Words are only seven percent of communication. The other ninety-three percent of communication involves what we can believe.

A tool that helps me to communicate with others is called Neuro Linguistic Programming or NLP. Richard Bandler developed this course and Anthony Robbins helped me adapt it to my life. According to the research done regarding NLP, there are three primary ways we communicate. At a very early age (some say as early as six months), each of us develops a style that is right for us. We feel most comfortable in this particular way of listening and communicating in our world. The three ways are visual, auditory and kinesthetic (meaning feeling). According to the research, the following statistics are typical for the American population:

Visual	55%
Auditory	10%
Feelings (kinesthetic)	35%

According to NLP research, more men are primarily visual than women; more women are primarily kinesthetic.

Characteristics of the Visual Person

Attains positions of influence (movers and shakers)
Displays high energy and vitality
Tends to appear arrogant
Prefers extremely mobile lifestyle
Speaks in high-pitched and strained tones
Vocalizes expressively (sometimes in quick bursts)

Shows enthusiasm in face and body
Holds tension in shoulders
Checks the rear-view mirror
    frequently when driving
Smiles easily
Prefers face-to-face meetings
Dresses in current styles
Appears lanky, with long waists and
    thin body or thin people in heavy
    bodies
Tends to have tight abdominal
    muscles
Rubs neck while thinking
Points to eyes or out in front of self
Releases emotions easily
Gestures with arms and hands while
    talking
Gets to the point ASAP
Gets the job done
Dislikes being humored

Visual words:

See	seeing	clarity
focus	imagine	image
magnified	shape	size
perspective	observe	look
looking	looks	picture
clear	clearer	goofy
vague	shiny	muted
see a pattern	color	colorful
see the light	bright	dim
enlightenment	cast some light	

A visual person enjoys:

TV	art collecting
galleries	reading
primping	movies
photography	window-shopping

Visual communicators often work in positions of leadership, such as president or executive director of a corporation, or leader of a club. Two other careers that work well for the visual person are landscape designer and architect.

Characteristics of the Auditory Person

Perceives sounds intensely (can be
   pure ecstasy or total madness)
Prepares response internally before
   speaking
Finds other sounds distracting
Emphasizes verbal communications
Spends extended periods of time with
   his/her inner talk
Speaks in appreciative tones of voice
Walks gracefully
Shows eagerness to hear another
   person's story
Feels extreme sensitivity to animals
Needs to live in quiet places with soft
   sounds such as streams or birds
Likes sound of own voice
Prefers less mobility than the visual
Walks with a flowing motion
Intellectualizes easily
Prefers lay therapists as friends
Talks in an elegant manner (monotone
   is a turn off)
Dominates conversations
Talks to self more than others
Tends to move lips while reading
Repeats back what he/she has heard
Mimics tone and pitch
Learns foreign languages easily
Learns by listening
Dresses sensibly (not fancy and not
   always in style)
Displays less tension than a visual
Has slimmer or more muscular build

than the kinesthetic
Points to ears often while explaining
    something
Tends to cup hands around ears
Desires harmony and loyal friends

Auditory Words:

sounds like	sounding	sound
talk	hear	tell me
tells	tune in	tune out
loud/soft pitch	tone	volume
noise	listen	rhythm
tempo	harmony	gun
rattling around	static	clicks
clear as a bell	negative ring	frequency
make beautiful music together		speaking

An Auditory Person Enjoys:

music	concerts
dancing (disco)	hearing lectures
radio	talking on the phone
CB radio	inner conversations
listening to the TV	eavesdropping
playing musical instruments	

Some careers that auditory people tend to choose include record producer, psychotherapist, orator, clergy, magician, peace maker and negotiator.

176

Characteristics of the Kinesthetic (Feeling) Person

Tends to be sentimental
Contemplates a problem from many
    different points of view
Shares a dialogue with anyone
    around them
Talks about a love affair long after it is
    over
Enjoys silence
Appears approachable and open
Needs to feel everything is in order
Holds breath when nervous
Enjoys tranquil, relaxing sounds such
    as Gregorian chants, whale
    sounds, wind chimes
Whispers secrets
Changes tone of voice
Internalizes everything
Senses physical surroundings more
    intensely than auditory or visual
Knows intuitively things that are
    hidden or unspoken
Recreates/recalls memories of joy,
    love, hurt, happiness, sadness
Loves to feel — needs tactile
    stimulation
Gives physical rewards
Interprets auditory's dialogue
Supplies the world with poetry
Makes decisions based on feelings
Refuses to be rushed in life
Uses conversations to transform
    words, sounds and images into
    feelings

Dislikes long meetings
Is well-loved
Dresses for comfort not style
Excels at manual tasks
Stands closer to people than others
Moves a lot
Learns by doing
Breathes slowly and deeply, low in
    stomach or diaphragm
Attaches sensations and feelings to
    experience
Empathizes easily; can replicate
    sensations of another's experience
Speaks reassuringly in deep tonality
    that inspire trust and confidence
Speaks slowly with long pauses
    (making the active visual
    impatient at times)
Enjoys muscle development, tends to
    be more muscular than auditory
Has fuller and softer bodies if not
    externally tactile
Takes the prize for being
    misunderstood, especially as
    being too emotional
Replaces one feeling with another
Tires easily
Soars like an eagle or experiences
    deep depression

Feeling words:

feel	understand	touch
keep in touch	hurt	warm
wet	dry	cold
exciting	ecstasy	bonding
keep abreast	close	sense
taste in mouth	sensitive	shook up
unbearable	reach out	hard
soft	comfortable	heavy
empathize	light-headed	location
moves me	shape	

A Feeling Person Enjoys:

laying in the sun	smoking	sailing
swimming	eating	running
dancing	cooking	drinking
weight-lifting	participating in sports	

Feeling people are often woodworkers, potters or massage therapists.

To build rapport with someone, you must communicate in their own language. The word rapport in Latin is *apportare* or *portare*, meaning to carry as a porter carries your bags. Dr. Albert Meherbain of UCLA reports that the nerve pathways of the eye to the brain are twenty-four times larger than the nerve pathways from the ear to the brain. The eye is the only sensory organ that contains brain cells.

Research found the visually-oriented person's eyes move up and to the right and left. The auditory person's eyes go to ear level. Ask a question of someone and watch their eyes to see

179

where they access information in their brain. A feeling person's eyes go down to the left. Watch for their response. A question could be: what is your home like? Listen to the answer and look at the eyes. A visual person will answer you by saying how the home looks. An auditory person will respond by telling you how it sounds. A feeling person will share with you how it feels. All are valid and contain powerful information for you.

A visual person takes shallow breaths from high in the chest, and may sound breathy. He or she may stop breathing when accessing pictures and lose some color in the face. When actually accessing an image, the visual person may flush.

An auditory person will typically have a regular and rhythmic flow of breath. The auditory person fills the chest area during inhalation. He has a projected exhalation, and may sigh in a more audible way. Usually this person is vocally precise in their use and inflections of speech and sound. This is different than the feeling person, who will usually breathe from the lower stomach area.

An angry visual person tends to clam up. When asked what their problem is, the usual response from the visual is to say nothing and walk away. When the auditory person is angry you can hear more than you want because of the loud talking. The feeling person wants to get physical or turns the anger inward. The feeling person may end up hitting, punching, or hurting himself or another person when angry.

Visual lovers like the lights on. They assume

their partner can "see" how they feel. They are very active and imaginative lovers. They may get carried away with how things look, rather than what is going on. They don't suppress their emotions easily. Visuals have feelings, but find it hard to express feelings in words.

The auditory lover responds to sound, whether it is the sound of a partner's voice, music, or background sounds. Do not say "I love you" in the same tone of voice all the time. The auditory lover wants to hear what is going on. They often like to talk while doing something physical. Your sounds are a great turn on for them, so never use a monotone voice.

Feeling lovers want the lights out, to heighten every sensation. Touching is central to their lovemaking, and kinesthetic communicators tend to be terrific in bed. Their miracle from God is emotion and feeling. In fact, feeling people get caught up in their own feelings so much during lovemaking, they sometimes forget about their partner. The touch of their partner can help to pull the feeling lover back into the love experience. The sensation of being grounded lingers for the feeling lover long after the situation is over. Physical touch is the way to reach the heart of the kinesthetic communicator.

When laughing, visual people tend to chuckle from their throat or chest level. Auditory people laugh from the solar plexus and waist level. Feeling people laugh from a place further down, near the navel and abdomen. You might hear their laughter called a "belly laugh."

As you learn what type of communicator you are, you can cross the bridge and talk to someone in *their* language to create rapport. When people are *like* each other, they tend to *like* each other. It is important to remember that the quality of life *is* the quality of your own communication skills. One definition I like for communication is:

Communication: The process of conveying information by language, signs, symbols and behavior to move toward an outcome.

Communication involves sharing, conveying knowledge or information, and making clear signs. Communication passes from one to another while receiving or transmitting. Communicating is an act of transmitting verbal, written or body messages. It is the process of exchanged messages. The power in good communication is not to control but rather set yourself free to exchange the energy of each other. The strongest communicator would develop all three modes of visual, auditory and feeling/kinesthetic. This blend puts you in greater rapport with the people that you want to communicate with.

If you discover that you are a visual person and the person you are communicating with is a feeling person, you can learn to talk to them in "their" language. This builds understanding with other people. When you first meet someone, you are on your best behavior. Later, when you become comfortable with that person, you return to your most comfortable way of communicating. This style preference starts very early in a person's life. Some researchers believe it starts before we are born, while we are still in the uterus.

Let's use an example of a visual woman and a feeling man who have had a very special evening planned for some time. The visual woman wants the place to look just right — she cleans so that everything sparkles. The windows will most likely be washed, even though dinner is in the evening. Candles are lit and flowers are on the table. The table is set with the best china and silver and it looks wonderful. The food is arranged very attractively on the plate. Most likely, the visual lady did not cook the food, but it will have a fine presentation on the plate. Her hair will be freshly coifed, and she will wear a new dress in the best color for her complexion. She looks stylish and radiant in the soft lighting of the room. Music can be heard, but is not loud enough to be distracting.

Seven o'clock is the agreed-upon time for this special dinner together. When 7:30 or 8 p.m. comes, the feeling man finally arrives, happy as a lark to see this visual lady. He picks her up and swings her around in an adoring hug, and tousles her hair with the joy he feels when near her. He soon realizes how quiet she is and asks, "Is everything all right?" Although she says yes, he knows it isn't. He explains that someone got a promotion at work. His office celebrated with one little drink, and in the excitement time just got away from him.

In his favorite sneakers and sweats, the feeling man is very comfortable and in a "feel good" mood. He even suggests they have a little fun in the bedroom before eating. Meanwhile, the visual woman is becoming quieter, although she still claims that nothing is wrong. Do you think this evening will be as enjoyable and fun as planned? Not unless one or both of them uses the tools of NLP to cross the bridge with words and actions that the other will understand.

If the feeling man realized how important it was to his woman that the entire environment was visually pleasing, perhaps he would have dressed up, and brought along a comfortable change of clothes for later. The feeler would have noticed how great the visual looked, and complimented her for taking the time and effort to make the table and home a picture of beauty. He would have brought her a small gift, something visual to show her in her own language how much she means to him. Later on, he would be sensitive to her romantic needs, and make sure the lights remained on during their lovemaking, to enhance the mood of this special evening. When he realized how tardy he was going to be, a phone call would have prepared her for the time delay.

In the same way, the visual lady could have communicated to the feeling man if she knew his language. She might have greeted him by name at the door with a big hug. Asking for an explanation of his late arrival during these moments of closeness would have anchored a sense of understanding with the feeling person. She might have acknowledged that her outfit was a bit too formal for wearing at home, and offered him a glass of wine to drink while she changed into something more casual. Both of these actions would have appealed to his comfort level. When it came time to eat, she might have decided to move dinner from the formal dining room to the coffee table in the living room. Sitting on the floor, she can touch him more easily. As she reaches across the table to pass a dish, she allows her fingertips to brush against his hand. She speaks to him using feeling words and stays closely tuned to his emotional signals.

He raves about the curried rice, and she offers him more. With the ultra-sensitive taste buds typical of his communication style, he loves food and the different textures of food in his mouth. He sometimes chews with his eyes closed, to savor the flavors more completely. The feeling man's senses are totally involved when it comes to food, lovemaking, and everything else in life. If he and she can build rapport and bridge the space between their communication styles, a great evening will reward them.

My daughter discovered that she was kinesthetic (feeling) when she scored twenty-eight out of thirty on a questionnaire. After that it was much easier for me to understand her. As a baby, she liked to be snuggled and held very close. After nursing, she was very happy just being held and rocked for long periods of time. When she came home from school, she always wanted to touch me or be near me. When she played by herself, she preferred being in the same room with me.

If I wore a piece of clothing made of soft fabric, she would stroke me as she sat or stood near me. I used to say, "Janine, just go play."

185

"But Mommy, I just want to touch you for awhile," she replied.

As a visual mother, I wanted Janine to wear pretty little dresses all the time. She didn't like that at all.

My son is high on the visual scale, so he responded to life in a different way. When he was a baby and finished nursing, he no longer wanted to be held. He pushed away from me, and wanted to be put down. Years later, when he came home from elementary school, he would open the refrigerator to see what was there — even if he wasn't hungry. He needed to see things. Sometimes, after coming into the house, he would just yell out, "Hi Mom, I'm home, where are you?" Sight and vision was important to him, and touch was not.

Both of my children joined the Air Force; they had very different reasons for doing so, and their reactions to being in military service were different. Since he was in the sixth grade, David's goal had been to attend the Air Force Academy. He did everything necessary to attain his goal, including making excellent grades. David received the appointment from his Congressperson with a 4.0 grade average from the high school he attended. He didn't pass the second physical because he was deaf on one side. As a visual person, when David was told he wasn't a perfect specimen of an American male, he dealt with his anger by becoming silent. He did not show his disappointment.

David then decided on another goal. After high school, he joined the Air Force because his college education would be paid. He hoped to teach at the Academy or for the Air Force. David loved the discipline of the service as well as looking good in the uniform. Always self-disciplined, David constantly worked toward a goal as visual people do.

Janine joined the Air force for the discipline and to get an education. Remember, Janine likes to feel good and wasn't overly concerned with her appearance. Janine hated the service. Her assigned duty was at the base hospital. Janine had a heightened sense of empathy with the patients at there, and she couldn't bear to see them suffering. She also couldn't bear the sight of someone's blood. Janine could "feel" the needle as if it was going into her and not just the patient. The sight of blood was a feeling sensation for her, not just a visual one. Janine became involved more deeply with the patient's pain than a visual or an auditory person would. When she got married and became pregnant with my first granddaughter, she opted out of the Air Force.

I know that my children took on their primary communication characteristics at a very young age. If I had understood these concepts when they were children, I could have adjusted their environments to help them be more satisfied and at ease. I also could have shared the information with their father, for him to use during the years that he raised them.

Knowing whether you are visual, auditory or

kinesthetic/feeling is a great advantage. You can become more aware of the various facets of your life, such as personal, social, and spiritual. For example, what types of prayer do you like? Do you prefer the visionary, where scenes are painted by the words that are spoken? Do you like the rhythm of the prayer, or the music or tone of the voice of the person speaking the prayers? Or is the most important thing the emotions and feelings that prayers evoke from you? Do you feel you communicate the best with the God of your understanding at the visual, auditory or feeling level? You will tend to choose a church that fulfills more of your communication needs, which means a church that speaks to you in your own language — your innate communication style. There is no right or wrong, just a difference of viewpoint.

When you ask your boss for a raise, if you ask in their language you are more likely to receive it. For example, if you work for a visual boss, keep your request short and to the point. Visuals are not sentimental, so don't waste your time telling sad stories about your personal needs concerning the raise. Make sure you are well-dressed and well-groomed when you go into his or her office. If the boss seems busy, ask for an appointment at a later time. Make sure you are on time. In fact, show up a little early. Visuals usually have their watches set ahead of time, so they won't be late. They tend to want everyone else to be like they are.

Smile occasionally during the meeting, but not excessively. Be friendly, but not too friendly. Shake the boss's hand, but just briefly. Get to the bottom line quickly and leave. Leave a brief written summary highlighting the factors that show you deserve the raise — this will give their visually-oriented brain a point of focus. Make sure you speak as fast as they do, and match their breathing pattern.

If your boss is auditory, compliment him on the pleasing music in his office, making sure you vary your speech pattern and tone of voice. Your attire should be sensible, and not necessarily fashionable. Usually no-nonsense shoes will impress an auditory boss.

If you have a feeling boss, explain in feeling words why you are a benefit to the company, and why you deserve the raise. The summary you leave with your boss must also be in feeling words. Tell several anecdotes to elicit empathy. Take deep breaths and breathe from the lower abdomen area. Take some extra care in your appearance on the day that you ask for a raise, but don't make extreme changes — they might make you look out of place in the feeling boss's office.

If you are a teacher (and we are all teachers at some point), teach in all three ways. To teach the visual, let the student see what you are teaching. When teaching the auditory, use music in the background and teach in a rhyme. When teaching feeling people, use hands-on exercises that allow the student to do and touch during the lesson. When you include techniques from all the three individualities, you are more assured of meeting the needs of all the learners.

When visual people set goals and dreams,

they are in pictures and usually in color. Auditory people hear someone telling them their dreams and goals have come true, in words and sounds of accomplishment and victory. Feeling people's goals and dreams can usually be sensed as a temperature or pressure change in the pit of their stomachs. To reach all levels of your being, experiment with experiencing your goals and dreams as already accomplished in all three forms. Be a magnet, attracting your goals and dreams into your life in an easy way.

NOT ALL IS GOOD, BUT
GOOD COMES FROM ALL.

Chapter 25

Co-Creation or Creation by Default

When we don't take total responsibility in our lives, we create by default. It may seem that things just happen to us, but that's not so — they happen through us. Vibrational matches are drawn into our lives. It is difficult to achieve goals and dreams when we create by default. Everyday activities are allowed to take priority, and then we simply react to them. On this path, we end up as talented firefighters, and we learn how to deal with crises (which seem to arise quite often). Wouldn't it be nice to dance with our goals and dreams instead?

When you turn toward recognizing a higher power, you become a co-creator of your life. Call that power God, the Universe, The Force, Infinite Intelligence or any other name. You create the pictures, sounds, and feelings that you would experience when your goals and dreams have been reached. In this way, whatever happens en-route to those goals and dreams, you realize you are the master of your destiny, not a victim of circumstances.

You create your life experience through your thoughts. In a literally sense, every thought that flashes through (or lingers) in your mind gives birth to a creation. Your vibration is creation in motion, and the intensity of your feelings increase the power of those vibrations. The more you wrap your emotions into a thought, the more likely you are to have eventual fulfillment of that thought. Even with little emotion, thinking a thought frequently enough creates it in your life. This process produces changes in the physical realm regardless of the thought.

The Universe is neutral and will manifest whatever you are thinking. *Every single thought has creative power!* The Universe (also known as God) gave you this creative tool to use to see in what direction you are headed. Are you going toward what you want or running away from what you don't want? The best measuring stick is the way you feel. Feeling good is the best tool for checking to see if you are going in the direction of your goals and dreams.

All thoughts create. The more emotion you engage, the faster the creation is manifested as reality in your life experience. When you experience deliberate creation, you are choosing the thoughts and feelings you want to manifest in your life. When you give thought to what you don't want, (and end up creating it anyway) this is creation by default.

For years, I created all the reasons why I couldn't write a book. I didn't know how. Who would be my editor? Who would publish it? Who would read it after it was published? Who had the time to do such a thing? What if I was punished for writing as I had been in another lifetime?

I was creating by default what I really didn't want. Deep in my heart and within my soul, I had to write for myself, if not for any other reason. Just do it — even if I couldn't answer the questions posed by my mind. Now you are reading something that I didn't know how to do until I employed deliberate creation and focused intention. In Unity, we say, "As you think, so you are." The Abraham material teaches the same principle in different words: "Want, allow it to be, and it is." A more precise term is intention. The law of creation could be phrased as, "Intend it, allow it, and it is."

Many times when we want something, we reverse the mindset that could help us acquire it by saying something like this: "I want a new white car, but it is too expensive." That is a perfect example of denying intention. You begin to acknowledge the intention, and then cancel it in the next breath, "It is too expensive. I can't afford it." Is it any surprise how often we create by default? It takes deliberate creation to truly become co-creative with the power of the energy that creates *all*.

Although we don't consciously create everything in our lives, we must take responsibility for our accidental creations. The earlier we recognize this, the sooner we can give up the role of victim. Playing victim is neither energizing nor fun. However, we may not know how to do anything else. We become used to a role. It is like an actor or an actress who gets type-cast in a particular genre and portrays the same kind of

193

person over and over again in movie after movie. Do we retreat into a comfort zone and become type-cast? Why not apply and prepare for the hero's role in your own life? All you need to do is learn new thoughts and feelings. You can become the hero or heroine you really are.

FEELINGS — FEAR OR LOVE?

You can choose what you feel. What you feel will tell you when you are in tune and on track. When you feel really good you are "in the flow." That is the place to remember and return to. When you allow the feeling of fear to take over, you are out of tune, off track and out of the flow of your desired good.

The emotions that you feel are always responding to the present moment. The past is gone. The future is not here. Today is a gift. That is why it is called the present. If fear is felt due to thoughts of the future, stop, look and see there is no basis for fear. Fear is False Evidence Appearing Real. Fear is Forgetting Everything is All Right. Put fear to the rear. Remember that everything is all right. You can alter the future by altering your present thoughts in the here and now moment. If you allow fear-based thoughts to continue, you are transmitting creative power in the wrong direction. You are handing your power over to what you fear. You are creating by default the very situations that you don't want to experience.

What do you choose? What do you want? How do you want to feel? Who has the power to change your mind? Realize that only you have the power to change your mind, and move toward what you want. No one else can do it for you. Not even Jesus Christ. You may think He will do it for you, but in fact, Jesus Christ does it through you. The truth is, at times we really want someone else to do it for us. It is at these times we need to be aware that there are a host of vibrational energies in the Universe to call upon for help.

To personalize my helpers, I call them my angels. I know they are there to help me. They can be everywhere at one time. While in my physical body, I think I am limited. I send my parking angel to find parking places. If I allow enough time for this, I get a space in a very convenient location. When I leave home to run errands, I can ask my parking angel to find a parking place right in front of the store, restaurant or library. When I arrive at my destination, my parking spot is waiting for me. I state my request one time, say thank you, and go about my journey. There are other times when I ask for a parking space when I'm just a block away, or even turning the corner at my destination. In those cases, I may or may not find a convenient space. But then, who didn't do the asking ahead of time?

You can do this too. There is nothing too trivial to ask. There is nothing so big that the Universe can't handle it. Have your prayerful intentions ahead of time in both the big and small aspects of your life.

Many people live in fear of the future. They may fear the unknown or the changes that are a natural part of life. They may fear future discomfort in their physical bodies or catastrophes caused by the weather. The way to relieve these anxieties is by relying on the power of the angels. To prevent yourself from attracting these negative situations to you, you can pre-plan by calling upon your angels. It is not enough to pray for your life to merely continue. Pray for your physical life to have joyous continuation. You want to be free with the freedom of spirit and filled with complete good. As we live life, some pain is inevitable. Whether or not we turn that pain into suffering is our choice.

I remember emerging from a dysfunctional relationship. During the aftermath, I seemed to be frozen in the past. I was always talking about what had happened, what a victim I had become, "if only" this, and "if only" that. I was really good at reliving the suffering of the relationship, and prolonging its drama. I told my sad story to everyone who showed even the slightest interest in the status of my life. When they asked how things were, I unloaded on them with the intimate and painful details. I was in the "if only" syndrome.

One day a friend told me: "Thelma, I don't want to pet your old dead cat anymore."

"What do you mean?" I asked. "I don't even have a cat, let alone a dead one." He responded, "Yes, you do. You are carrying that dead relationship around your neck asking everyone to pet your old dead cat. I am not going to do it anymore."

That picture was a very vivid one for me. I saw an image of a big black cat that had gotten stiff from being dead for so long. There I was, walking through life with the cat around my neck. When someone asked a question about me or my situation I would ask them to pet my old, dead, black, stiff "cat" while I told them the full story of my unhappy life. Cats shed their fur even when alive so just imagine how a dead stiff cat would shed its fur with this very vivid image.

It was time to change. I wanted to release myself from the old dead cat. Even more, I wanted to remove the cat fur that had stuck to me and my clothes and my life. What had happened was, the more I told my sad, sad story, the more fur (old negative energy) stuck to me.

My first step was to plan a response to people who asked about my situation. Here is what I came up with: "Oh, things are really getting a lot better. I feel myself healing. I really can see a light at the end of the tunnel — and it is not a freight train coming at me." After saying that, I would smile and change the subject. The easiest way to do that was to ask people about their lives. People enjoy talking about themselves. Sometimes I would recognize people talking about their old dead cat, but at least it wasn't my dead cat anymore.

Now when I seem to be obsessed about something I just ask myself, "Is this an old dead cat — something that I want to get rid of?" It's an easy way for me to check on myself. Many times I have to call upon my Higher Power to help me remove an old dead cat. Some things seem easier than others to release. For those things that are harder to release, I request help from the angels that God

197

has sent to me. I become willing to "let God and let go." In order to let go, we need an understanding of what we want to release. After we first "let God," then the foundation exists to "let go." Trust is required. First, we trust that the universal power takes care of our lives. Then we can "let go" to that power. As my friend, Dr. Jerry Jampolsky says in his book: "Love is letting go of fear." To truly let go of fear without clinging to the problem, you must feel the presence of love.

TRANSFORMING NEEDS AND WANTS — CREATING THE DESIRE TO HAVE

I believe we never get something that we need. However, we do get what we desire and prefer in our lives. In speaking the words "I need," I separate myself from what I want. If I say, "I need to stop smoking," unless I have the desire to do so, I won't do it. The term "need" is a spiritual handcuff to the problem. However, when a person makes the decision to stop smoking or drinking, the whole Universe comes to support that decision. Sometimes that support manifests as relief of the body's physical addiction. Sometimes it means discovering a support group that gives verbal, mental, emotional, and spiritual support. Support may come in the form of counseling, a doctor, a hospital, or a nicotine patch. After making the decision, all types of support will be available to help you accomplish your desired goal.

Remember, as long as you "need" something you don't or won't get it. If I say I need a new car, it implies there must be something wrong with my old one. If I say I want a new car, this subtle difference in phrasing thinking affects the mind. That sets up the intention, the vibration, to create a situation in which a new car is a reality. Declare a statement such as, "I have decided to get a new car." Friends begin to ask you about your desire. What kind of car? What color? What style? As you talk with others, they think about you driving the car you want. Their thoughts are aligned with your thoughts to support your desire. They may even know where you can get a great deal. But as long as you need a car, people's thoughts focus on the problems of your old car. This creates a separation — a vibrational match of what you don't want. This is called praying against you.

When recovering from an addiction, as long as we *need* to be free, we are not naming and claiming our freedom. We handcuff the bondage of addiction to us. We keep returning to the problem because we haven't decided to be free of the addiction. This process also applies to being overweight. As long as we need to lose weight, we never will. When we have decided to lose weight, we become slim and trim. It is important to eliminate weight in a healthy and joyous way. Many of us have made dieting an ordeal involving deprivation. The first three letters of diet are die. Since we resist dying, we resist dieting from the core of our being. When we make a conscious decision to be slim, trim, healthy, pretty, or handsome we experience an inner change. "Nothing tastes as good as slim feels" is a highly motivating statement for me.

When I was at a point in my life I refer to as

199

my pothole of insanity, I gained forty pounds in a short period of time. This weight gain was tied to my anger and stuck emotions. I went on starvation diets and even fainted from malnutrition. I joined a program, and after a weigh-in one time I decided I wasn't losing weight quickly enough. After I fainted and ended up in a hospital emergency room, I knew there had to be a better way. I joined a group of people who supported me in eliminating my outer weight as I dealt with my stuck emotions. Once I did this, the weight came off, easily. To this day, I do not own a scale, and I weigh myself just once a month. Since 1983, I have been within my desired weight range. I wear from size two to eight. When I wear size eight, it is because I like lots of room in my clothes.

I couldn't lose weight while resisting the reality of my life. I found myself feeling miserable. Then I decided to have fun by losing weight in a healthy way. By dealing with the root cause and the stuck emotions, I was forever changed. I even let myself eat my fear food. You know what your fear food is. It's the one that makes you think, "Well, here adds another pound or two," every time you eat it.

My mother used to say, "Just smelling food I gain weight." Obesity is my family dis-ease. Most members of my family deal with excess bodyweight. It can be tempting to blame out-of-control fat cells on heredity. My fear food was ice cream. For thirty days, I ate ice cream every single day, smothered in nuts and toppings of all kinds. At the end of thirty days of facing my fear food and taking the power away from it, I had lost weight.

Find your fear food. Make peace with it. Take your power back, naming, claiming, and accepting your ideal healthy body weight.

Every time I bless the food I eat, I name and claim my ideal, healthy body weight. I actually name the pounds as I speak the blessing. I claim I am eating pure light, because everything I put into my mouth comes from the Light. I hold my hands over the food as I bless it, because blessed food is assimilated better — with more energy in a useable form — for the physical temple called the body. After all, our bodies are the temples of the mind, and both need to be given food.

NOT ALL IS GOOD, BUT
GOOD COMES FROM ALL.

Chapter 26

The Final Chapter

There is never a final chapter, because we are always at the beginning. Beginning of something, beginning of the first day of the rest (best) of our lives. You picked up this book for a reason. This message comes with love, an *unconditional* love. Like the love my mother had for me, even before I was born. Like the love of the man who married her; the one that I called Father during my childhood. Like the love I found for myself during my search of becoming who I am. The love of God that is inside this book.

Let your life begin with the lessons in this book and allow God to reveal additional ways for you to discover the amazing potential of who you are. Start asking questions, trust your intuition and search out people to guide you to why you came into to this lifetime. Learn how to express the You.

First, trust in spirit (God) as I did many times. Spirit used many avenues of supply for my children and me. God is my Source — the avenue or channel varies.

Second, learn from Chapter 16. This is the

process for healing. It may be a healing of emotions, physical or mental, as well as spiritual and the process works.

Third, have fun. Chapter 17 shows you how to treasure map. Make it a wonderful fun way of prayer to manifest your dreams.

Fourth, know the power of your spoken word. How powerful our words and desires are. They affect those you speak about as well as yourself. Work with Chapter 25 and become a co-creator.

Finally, Love yourself. This is the message Jesus brought us from God. And this is the message God sends to us everyday with various messengers. Find whatever you call your Higher Power, be it God, Goddess, or All That Is. The message from the beginning is You are loved, living, lovable, love-filled, and love overflowing.

Scripture time and time again says: Love is the fulfillment of the law. (Romans 13:10)

But the fruit of the Spirit is love, joy, peace, patience, kindness, goodness, faith, and modesty. (Galatians 5:22)

God is Love. (John 1:3)

There are so many other wonderful messages to explore through books and people you meet on your path. May your Journey be a blessed one.

NOT ALL IS GOOD, BUT
GOOD COMES FROM ALL.

This book was typeset to accommodate the visual needs of a variety of readers. The body text font is Versailles (11.75 point). Extra space was added between the lines and between paragraphs to enhance readability. The author welcomes your feedback regarding this layout.

This is the first edition, and although it was proofed many times, errors may still exist. Please contact the author to report your findings. Thank you for your help!

Reverend Thelma J. Hembroff c/o
Unity of Cedar Rapids
3791 Blairs Ferry Road N.E.
Cedar Rapids, IA 52402